LLANDUDNO LIFEBOATS

AN ILLUSTRATED HISTORY OF LIFEBOATS AT LLANDUDNO, LLANDDULAS AND CONWY

Nicholas Leach

FOXGLOVE PUBLISHING

First published 2018, updated 2019

Published by
Foxglove Publishing Ltd
Foxglove House, Shute Hill,
Lichfield WS13 8DB
United Kingdom
Tel 07940 905046

ISBN 9781909540125

Typesetting, design and layout by
Nicholas Leach/Foxglove Publishing

Printed by Hobbs the Printers Ltd, Totton,
Hampshire, SO40 3WX.

Cover: Llandudno's Shannon class lifeboat
William F. Yates. (Nicholas Leach)

Page 1: Llandudno's lifeboats William F. Yates
and Dr Barbara Saunderson on exercise off the
promenade. (Nicholas Leach)

Left: One of the old service boards now on
display inside the lifeboat house.

Contents

Acknowledgements

Many people have assisted with this project to produce a comprehensive history of the Llandudno lifeboat station, and I am very grateful to them all. In particular, I extend my considerable gratitude to Deputy Launching Authority Alun Pari Huws, who not only got the project started but has been involved at every stage, answering many questions unstintingly, providing hundreds of photographs and interesting images for possible inclusion, and generally assisting in every way possible. Without his input, this book could not have been written.

It is not easy to accurately credit all the photographs as their origins are not always known, but every effort has been made to identify photographers. Particular thanks are due to John Lawson-Reay, local historian and former shore crew, for permission to use a number of his images; to Joan Hughes, wife of the late Hughie Hughes, a crew member for thirty-seven years; to Edith Bellamy, wife of the former Coxswain Gordon Bellamy; to the family of the late Terry Taylor; to Amy Haywood Francis, three generations of whose ancestors were crew members; and to the late Christmas Tudno Jones, former Second Coxswain, for items from his collection.

Thanks are due to a number of station personnel for their input and support, particularly Coxswain Graham Heritage; Mechanic Les Jones; Head Launcher and former Coxswain Ian (Dan) Jones; Station Training Co-ordinator and former Coxswain Robin Holden; Lifeboat Operations Manager Marcus Elliott; and Press Officer Alan Sharp. The staff of Conwy Council Archives office are also acknowledged for their interest and assistance.

Previous accounts of the station's history, written by Aled Eames in 1961 for the station's centenary and by Jeff Morris in 1991, provided much source material, and gratefully acknowledged. For the chapter on Conwy, thanks are due to Lifeboat Operations Manager Aled Williams, Helm Danny-Lee Davies and their station colleagues some of whom have been involved since the station opened in 1965.

At the RNLI Headquarters in Poole, thanks to Nathan Williams at the Film and Imaging Unit; Roger Aldham; and the RNLI Heritage Team, notably Hayley Whiting and Joanna Bellis, who continue to facilitate my research. John Harrop and Iain Booth supplied old postcards; Tony Denton, Martin Fish and Phil Griffiths supplied photos; Bryan Hughes read through various chapters; and Brian Bell, owner of the old lifeboat house at Llanddulas, kindly allowed many of his old photos to be included; my gratitude extends to them all.

Nicholas Leach, Lichfield, February 2018

About the author

Nicholas Leach has a long-standing interest in lifeboats and the lifeboat service. He has written many articles, books and papers on the subject, including a history of the origins of the lifeboat service; a comprehensive record of the RNLI's lifeboat stations in 1999, the organisation's 175th anniversary; RNLI Motor Lifeboats, a detailed history of the development of powered lifeboats; and numerous station histories, including ones covering the Welsh stations of Moelfre, Holyhead and Porthdinllaen. He has visited all of the lifeboat stations in the UK and Ireland, past and present, and is Editor of Ships Monthly, the international shipping magazine.

Forewords

Dedication by Lord Mostyn

My family have been involved with Llandudno lifeboat station since it was established in 1861 with several members holding offices in station management and the Ladies Guild. It therefore gives me great pleasure to dedicate this book to everyone, past and present, who have committed so much of their time and energy to saving life at sea around this part of the North Wales coast. As the station enters an exciting and long awaited new chapter in its history, I wish all its volunteers success in preventing loss of life, safety in all they do and satisfaction in their work.   *Mostyn*

From the Lifeboat Operations Manager

I first became involved with Llandudno lifeboat through a Lifeboat Youth Guild in my teenage years and, following several years away at sea, was delighted to join the station as a Deputy Launching Authority in 2000, becoming Lifeboat Operations Manager in 2003.

Llandudno lifeboat station may not have won many awards or been involved in famous rescues but, as this book illustrates, it is strategically located to protect people from the many marine hazards of the area and the surprisingly vicious local conditions which bad weather can create. It has saved many lives since it was established and will continue to do so. The station's crews and shore management teams have long gone about their voluntary work in a quiet, professional manner without fuss and it is a privilege for me to lead a well-drilled team.

With the construction of our new lifeboat house on the promenade, we now have a greatly enhanced capability to save lives at sea and train our dedicated volunteer crews to operate the technically advanced and versatile Shannon class lifeboat. We are also better able to engage with our supporters and the wider community. We look forward to continuing the long tradition of lifesaving in Llandudno.

Captain Marcus Elliott, Lifeboat Operations Manager

From the Chairman

Being involved in the lifeboat service is a way of life, often passed from one generation to another, as is illustrated in this book. It is consuming and requires the dedication and commitment from crews, management team and supporters, particularly in these days of comprehensive training and increasing regulatory obligations. It has been a privilege and pleasure for me to be involved with the station as station doctor since 1994, a fundraiser and, since 2011, Chairman.

I am grateful to well-known lifeboat author Nicholas Leach, supported by Alun Pari Huws, one of the Deputy Launching Authorities, for producing this fine record of Llandudno lifeboat station, as well as the work of Conwy and Llanddulas lifeboats. I hope you enjoy reading it and will be inspired to support the work we do, for without public support, we cannot function.

Dr J.J. Green, Chairman

Llandudno lifeboat station personnel

(As at 31 December 2018)

Lifeboat crew

Coxswain • Graham Heritage

Second Coxswain • Tim James

Assistant Coxswains • Dave Davis, Les Jones

Station Mechanic • Les Jones

Assistant Mechanics • Graham Heritage, Luke Heritage, Les Howell, Aled Williams

Inshore Lifeboat Helms • Simon Hajahmed, Luke Heritage, Phill Howell, Andy Jones

Crew • Simon Adey-Davies, Ian Appleton, Ewa Bajerska, Kelsey Byrne, Adam Finch-Saunders, Simon Hajahmed, Phill Howell, Andy Jones, Dave Jones, Mike Jones, Mark Lister, Lukasz Marchiniak, Chris Martin, Dave Roberts, Robbie Shields, Bert Williams and Jonathan Woodhead

Shore crew

Principal Head Launcher • Dan Jones MBE

Principal Tractor Driver • Ralph Hughes

Launch and Recovery Crew • Barney Baker, Keith Charlton, Sue Davies, Robin Fitzpatrick, Robin Holden, Steve Howard, Geraint Jones and John Roberts

Station management

Lifeboat Operations Manager • Captain Marcus Elliott

Deputy Launching Authorities • Mike Knowles, Paul Moreton, Alun Pari Huws

Lifeboat Station Chairman • Dr J.J. Green

Lifeboat Press Officer • Jonathan Coe

Deputy Lifeboat Press Officer • Luke Heritage

Lifeboat Training Co-Ordinator • Robin Holden

Deputy Lifeboat Training Co-ordinator • John Roberts

Lifeboat Medical Advisor • Dr J.J. Green

Lifeboat Treasurer/Admin Officer • Arthur Barlow

Lifeboat Visitors Officer • Myfanwy Jones

Lifeboat Station Chaplain • Canon Philip Barratt

Llandudno and its maritime connections

Llandudno, styled 'Queen of the Welsh Resorts' in the nineteenth century, is the largest seaside resort in Wales. The town was developed during the second half of the 1800s as a holiday resort after Owen Williams, an architect and surveyor from Liverpool, presented Lord Mostyn with plans to develop the marshlands behind Llandudno Bay. These were enthusiastically pursued by Lord Mostyn, and the influence of the Mostyn Estate and its agents has been crucial in the development of the town, especially after George Felton was appointed as architect in 1857.

The town and surrounding coastline is dominated by the Great Orme's Head, which protrudes into Liverpool Bay and the Irish Sea. Formed of limestone, it overshadows its smaller sister, the Little Orme's Head, and views from it show both the beauty and potential marine hazards of the area. To the north–west lies Anglesey with its neighbouring lifeboat stations of Beaumaris (Atlantic 85) and Moelfre (Tamar and D class inflatable), both of which are just visible in clear weather.

To the west lies the entrance to the Menai Strait, which effectively starts at Ynys Seiriol/Puffin Island to the east and

A view looking west over Llandudno Bay and the North Shore, a beach of sand, shingle and rock, curving for two miles between the headlands of the Great Orme and the Little Orme, with the lifeboat house completed in 2017 at Craig-y-Don in the foreground. (Nicholas Leach)

The coaster Carrier aground at Llanddulas pier in 2012; when the lifeboat launched to her aid, getting away from the North Shore was particularly challenging and required the utmost skill on the part of the coxswain to time the launch from the carriage. Due to the conditions, recovery was undertaken at the West Shore, which offered slightly greater shelter from the northerly gale. Prior to this, launches or recoveries at the West Shore were very rare, although exercises were undertaken there at times.

narrows across the broad and dangerous Lafan Sands past Beaumaris to the strong tidal currents of the 'Swellies' between the Menai Suspension and Britannia Bridges before continuing to Caernarfon and the sea beyond. To the south of the Great Orme lie the dangerous sandbanks of the Conwy estuary with its one main and one secondary channel leading in and out of the small historic port, which is also home to Llandudno's flank ILB station (D class inflatable) at Conwy's town quay. To the east lies the rocky coastline of Penrhyn Bay and Rhôs on Sea, before the sandy beaches of Colwyn Bay.

Also to the east of Colwyn Bay can be found the jetty at Llanddulas, where coasters regularly visit to load locally quarried limestone; a mile to the west, between 1869 and 1932, a lifeboat was also operated. Beyond this lie the long sandy beaches of Pensarn, Towyn, Rhyl and Prestatyn. Rhyl's lifeboat station (Mersey and D class inflatable, 13m Shannon due 2019) is supplemented by an RNLI Lifeguard team during the summer at this popular holiday resort. Out to sea lie three wind farms: Rhyl Flats (twenty-four turbines), Gwynt y Môr (160) and, in the distance, close to Hoylake lifeboat station's operating area, Hoyle Bank (thirty).

The lifeboat station at Llandudno was founded in 1861 and the volunteer crews have been saving lives at sea for well over 150 years. After operating the lifeboat from a carriage and launching at Llandudno's North Shore, either from the slipway by gravity or by launching falls (a traditional system of ropes on the lifeboat's carriage designed to haul the boat into the water) from the beach, major changes took place during 2017. An impressive new lifeboat house was completed at Craig-y-Don, just to the west of the Little Orme headland, and a new 13m Shannon class lifeboat was placed on station, with its faster and safer bespoke launch and recovery system. This revolutionary new boat and launch vehicle not only brought operations into the modern era, but also closed a significant chapter in the history of the station, with the withdrawal from the Lloyd Street boathouse in the centre of town, the ending of the lifeboat being brought through the streets, and the use of falls for launching and skids for recovery.

Nicholas Leach and
Alun Pari Huws
March 2018

Nineteenth Century Pulling Lifeboats

L landudno lifeboat station was established in 1861 during a time when the Royal National Lifeboat Institution (RNLI) was expanding its operations. The RNLI was founded in 1824 through the efforts of Isle of Man-based baronet Sir William Hillary. His intention was to organise a national lifeboat service, but only after reforms of the Institution in the early 1850s was a truly national service possible. A lack of funds, due to insufficient appeals to the public, had hampered the work of the nascent Institution, and not until the second half of the nineteenth century did Hillary's original aim begin to be realised. By then, many seaside towns were sufficiently large and well developed to be able to provide a crew, all volunteers, to man a lifeboat, with some also having a fund-raising committee to help with financial matters.

Prior to the founding of the lifeboat station, attempts were made to improve the safety of shipping along the North Wales coast, where shipwrecks were not uncommon. Among the many ships wrecked was the brig *Hornby*, which was driven helplessly before a fierce north-westerly storm on New Year's Day 1824, ending up close to the rocks under Great Orme. Fourteen persons were on board, including two passengers and a cargo valued at £60,000. When the brig came ashore, one seaman, John Williams, was aloft, securing part of the rigging. The roll of the vessel in the heavy seas took him abreast of a ledge on the cliffs and he jumped across to safety as the brig backed off. The vessel was badly damaged by the impact and a few minutes later, in deep water, foundered, going down with thirteen left aboard. The incredibly fortunate John Williams clambered up the cliff, going from ledge to ledge, and reached part of the old copper mine workings on the Orme. His appearance is said to have startled the miners there, understandable given the circumstances. Following this incident, Williams never went to sea again, spending the rest of his life working in the Llandudno mines instead.

In 1845 the newly-built iron steamer *Engineer*, working a regular service carrying passengers and cargo between Liverpool and the

Menai Strait, broke her crankshaft during one of her voyages. She was left helpless in the face of a strong north-westerly gale and was in great danger close to the Orme, being pounded by rough seas as she was pushed steadily shorewards. Fortunately the signals of distress she sent up were seen by another steamer, *Cambria*, which got a rope aboard and took *Engineer* in tow, as far as Beaumaris. But for this providential help, *Engineer* would undoubtedly have been dashed to pieces at the foot of the Orme cliffs, with little hope of any of her numerous passengers and crew being saved.

Two years later the Italian two-masted brig *Archiduco Palatino* was driven ashore at Llandudno, against the cliffs on the site of the present Grand Hotel, during a severe gale. Scores of people watched her going ashore and a local boat, *Lady Harriet*, went out to try and give assistance. But the small boat capsized in the enormous waves breaking on the beach, with the loss of some of her crew. Meanwhile, eight of the eleven men aboard *Archiduco Palatino* put to sea in their own boat, but this too was overturned and sank drowning three people on board. The remaining five were saved thanks to the gallant efforts of the people ashore, as were the three who remained on the brig until the tide had receded.

These and other wrecks spurred efforts to safeguard shipping in the area. In 1815 the Trustees of the Liverpool Docks Committee provided a life-saving apparatus at Great Orme, and in 1859 a lighthouse was established on the Great Orme. It was built at the extremity of the headland, which jutted two miles out to sea, and was 300ft above sea level. Built by the Mersey Docks and Harbour Board, successors to the Liverpool Docks Committee, it proved to be a great help to the ships making for and departing from Liverpool, as well as the numerous smaller coasting craft using other the ports in the area. Proposals were also put forward to build some kind of harbour on the North Wales coast, where,

A generic illustration of the RNLI's standard self-righter of the late nineteenth century. Llandudno's first lifeboat would have been more or less identical in form.

The lighthouse on the Great Orme was one of a chain of lights along the coast of North Wales, guiding shipping along the Mersey channel. (From an old postcard supplied by John Mobbs)

according to a Parliamentary Select Committee appointed in 1836 to investigate the inadequacy of shelter for shipping making for Liverpool, 'there is a great deficiency of harbours of refuge'. Under one scheme, a ninety-acre harbour was proposed. It would have been linked to a railway terminus on the site of the present Grand Hotel, but nothing came of it and no harbour was built.

In November 1859 the first initiatives were made to establish a lifeboat station at Llandudno. The second half of the nineteenth century was the heyday of the 'standard' self-righting lifeboat, and Llandudno was served by a series of these craft. Self-righters were primarily rowing boats, usually 34ft or 35ft in length, and with a rather limited radius of action which meant stations were often established in close proximity to one another. The design had been perfected since its introduction in 1851 so that by the 1880s it was almost the only type of lifeboat in use. The six pulling lifeboats that served at Llandudno from 1861 until 1933, when motor lifeboats took over, were all self-righters.

By the late 1850s Llandudno was beginning to develop from a small village, consisting of a group of cottages occupied by copper miners and fishermen, into a seaside resort. The only shipping activities at Llandudno itself involved small craft unloading their cargoes on the beach when the tide was out. However, out to sea there was a steadily growing number of craft plying the shipping lanes to and from the burgeoning port of Liverpool. Many of the deepwater sailing vessels caught in adverse winds were driven off course towards the lee shore of North Wales, where the Great Orme presented the worst hazard eastward of Anglesey's rockbound shores. The nearest lifeboats to Llandudno at this time were at Rhyl, nearly seventeen miles to the eastwards, and at Penmon to the west, and many inhabitants of Llandudno were aware of the lack of facilities for lifesaving in the vicinity. This prompted the Rev M. Morgan and John Jones to write to the RNLI in November 1859 to state the necessity for a lifeboat.

The RNLI sent an Inspector of Lifeboats to assess the situation and he reported very favourably on what he found. His first visit to the town was on 7 July 1860 and he returned on 18 July 1860 to attend a public meeting at which it was resolved to form a Branch of the RNLI and formally request a lifeboat be stationed in the town. The RNLI's Committee of Management, at their meeting in London on 2 August 1860, agreed to the request, and plans were put in place to get a station established.

More or less coinciding with this, in 1860, the RNLI were presented with a gift of £200 from the Misses Brown of Toxteth Park, Liverpool, with the stipulation that it should go towards the cost of a lifeboat to serve Great Orme. The three sisters were frequent visitors to Llandudno and during their stays must have listened to, and been impressed by, tales of shipwrecks along this coast. In 1860, when one of the sisters died, the other two decided to donate the cost of a lifeboat to the RNLI in her memory.

With money for a lifeboat available, plans were put in hand to build a lifeboat house, and a site close to the railway station was offered to the RNLI by the Hon William Mostyn who, together with Edward Mostyn and architect and surveyor Owen Williams, had been involved in much of the planning and development of the town since the 1850s, and they were responsible for its expansion as a holiday resort.

A new boathouse was built at a cost of £147 10s 0d, and it was ready for the new boat, which was sent from London by rail on 11 January 1861, being conveyed free of charge by the London and North Western Railway Company. The Peake self-righting type, measuring 32ft by 7ft 10in, had been completed by Forrest at Limehouse, in London, at a cost of £190. The launching carriage, constructed by Robinson, cost a further £89.

The lifeboat and all her gear arrived at Llandudno on 15 January 1861. The formal inauguration of the new station, as well as the formal christening of the lifeboat, took place three days later. It was a major event for the town, and the afternoon was declared a general holiday. Shops and schools were closed, streets were decorated with bunting, and people from the surrounding area joined the townsfolk at the station square. There the lifeboat stood on her carriage, her new paintwork resplendent, dressed overall with flags and a large ensign.

With the crew on board the boat, the procession set off through the town for the beach, with the lifeboat drawn by a team of horses and her crew aboard, oars held high. Behind her came the local committee, led by the secretary John Williams. Then, in a succession of carriages, came Lady Mostyn and her party, with a guard of honour formed by the Seventh Caernarvonshire Volunteer Rifles. Between ranks of school children waving flags and thousands of cheering spectators, the procession reached the shore. There, Lady Mostyn christened the lifeboat in traditional fashion, smashing a bottle of wine over the stern, and then *Sisters Memorial* was launched. It was a cold but sunny afternoon and the new lifeboat had ideal conditions in a choppy sea with a stiff north-easterly breeze to show her paces in the bay. The opening of the station at Llandudno, according to *The Lifeboat* of 1 July 1861, 'completes the series of lifeboat stations on the north coast of Wales, for the protection of the immense shipping trade sailing to and from the great port of Liverpool'.

The first coxswain at Llandudno was Hugh Jones, a copper miner, who remained in the post until 1876. In the event of a service call when he was at work underground, the duty of calling him fell to his daughter, who had to run up to the mine where a special signal rapped down the shaft told her father that his crew was being summoned for a launch.

Sisters Memorial was on station for only six years, during which time she launched seven times and is credited with saving eight lives. Her first service took place on 9 February 1861, when she was tasked to a vessel which was in distress near Rhyl but was drifting west towards Llandudno in the face of a severe north-easterly gale. However, just before the lifeboat was launched, a message was received stating that the ship, the schooner *William*, of Liverpool, had sunk, and her five crew had been saved by the Rhyl lifeboat. However, the gale continued unabated throughout that night and the next morning another schooner went aground, on the Dutchman's Bank at the entrance to the Menai Strait, and this time *Sisters Memorial* was launched. The Penmon lifeboat, a small 28ft self-righter, was also called out and, being nearer the casualty, reached the scene first, finding the schooner *Village Maid*, of Fleetwood, in trouble. The Penmon lifeboat saved her four crew, and the *Sisters Memorial* was recalled.

The first effective service came later in 1861, on 13 September, when the flat *Uncle Tom*, of Runcorn, laden with coal, got into difficulties in heavy seas and a south-westerly gale. When she lost most of her sails, the crew dropped anchor off Llandudno, but, during the afternoon, the anchor began to drag and Sisters Memorial was launched. The lifeboat crew stood by until a tug arrived on the scene to tow the flat to safety.

The first life-saving service came on 7 December 1864, when *Sisters Memorial* was launched to the flat *Morning Star*, of Caernarfon, which had anchored near the Little Orme and hoisted a distress signal. She had lost her mast in heavy seas and a south-westerly gale. The lifeboat got alongside the vessel and saved the three crew, bringing them safely ashore. *Morning Star* survived the storm and was eventually taken into port and repaired, and continued to trade along the North Wales coast. Coincidentally, the next service launch by *Sisters Memorial* was to the same vessel. On 27 February 1866, while on passage from Port Dinorwic to Liverpool, with a

Believed to be the second Sisters Memorial lifeboat, on her launching carriage, on the Promenade. (By courtesy of Llandudno RNLI)

cargo of slate, *Morning Star* again got into difficulties off the Little Orme. The lifeboat crew had a considerable struggle to get *Sisters Memorial* close to the casualty, which had already sunk, forcing her three crew to take to the rigging. Eventually the lifeboat got close enough to rescue the men, and they were landed at Llandudno.

On 7 February 1867 the Llandudno volunteers were involved in an accident, which could have proved fatal, when their lifeboat capsized. *Sisters Memorial* was launched in a north-westerly gale after a ship was seen to be in distress off the Great Orme. The lifeboat crew had a hard struggle to get away from the shore and out of the Bay in the extremely heavy seas. As they neared the casualty, they found a tug already on scene. The tug had managed to get a line aboard the vessel and was towing it to safety. So the lifeboat was turned round and made for home but, in the appalling conditions, could make little progress back towards the beach. Coxswain Jones therefore decided make for the shelter of the mouth of the River Clwyd and headed for Rhyl.

Under a single double-reefed sail, *Sisters Memorial* battled across the open bay. However, when only about a mile away, she was struck by an exceptionally heavy wave and capsized. All but one of the crew were washed overboard, but after she had quickly righted herself all regained the boat or were pulled back aboard, wet but otherwise unhurt. Eventually they reached the shelter of Rhyl and clambered ashore, wet through and shaken by their experience, helped by some of the Rhyl crew who met them. The heavy weather continued and to save a long hard voyage home against the wind, the launching carriage arrived with a team of horses from Llandudno and the lifeboat was hauled back to her station by land. An official enquiry was held later to find the cause of the capsize. In the opinion of Coxswain Jones, the lifeboat was 'too sharp forward' and had insufficient beam, 'rendering her liable to be swamped and capsize'. She was clearly not suited to the task, and a new boat was required, as the RNLI acknowledged.

A larger lifeboat

As the accident had demonstrated that the lifeboat was too small and light for the station, the RNLI put in place plans to supply a larger lifeboat. The new boat was a 33ft by 8ft 7in ten-oared self-righter, then the standard type being built in large numbers, and was built by Forrestt at Limehouse at a cost of £284 3s 10d, and a new launching carriage, which cost £101, was also supplied. The new boat was given the same name as her predecessor in recognition of the original donors, one of whom had passed away since making their initial donation, and she arrived on station in July 1867, less than six months after the capsize.

The second *Sisters Memorial* served for just over twenty years, during which time she saved thirty-five lives and her services were much in demand, with her crew mainly helping smacks and flats, the small coastal trading vessels prevalent during the latter half of the nineteenth century. The first service took place in September 1867 when the smack *Jane*, on a passage to Runcorn from Caernarfon with slate, was dismasted in a northerly gale, six miles north of the Great Orme. The master, his wife and two of the crew were taken off just as the steamer *Prince Arthur*, returning to Liverpool from Menai Bridge, arrived on the scene. In view of the hard struggle facing the lifeboatmen on their trip back, *Prince Arthur* towed both smack and lifeboat close to Llandudno.

On 1 December 1867 *Sisters Memorial* was launched to the assistance of the smack *Brothers*, of Beaumaris, which was dragging her anchors in very heavy seas and a northerly gale. To get to the casualty as quickly as possible, the lifeboat was launched with only three of her regular crew of thirteen on board. Unfortunately, as the lifeboat came clear of her carriage, she was caught in the heavy surf and swept broadside back onto the beach. All her crew got ashore safely, but while the lifeboat was being pulled clear of the breakers, Coxswain Jones and six other men launched another boat and succeeded in reaching *Brothers*, shortly before she struck the rocks. They saved her two crew and brought them safely ashore.

Sisters Memorial was launched on 4 November 1869 to the

Llandudno's second lifeboat, Sisters Memorial, on her carriage outside the original boathouse next to the railway station. The crew are sitting in the boat wearing their cork life-jackets. The station was known as Orme's Head Lifeboat Station until 1892. (By courtesy of the RNLI)

Dutch brigantine *Catharina*, which had sailed from Runcorn a day or so previously with a cargo of salt destined for Riga in the Baltic. She was being driven towards the shore in Llandudno Bay by heavy seas in a north-westerly gale. The five crew were rescued and bought ashore, with the brigantine becoming a total wreck. One of the many people who witnessed this rescue was Lady Augusta Mostyn, who had christened Llandudno's first lifeboat in 1861. She was so impressed by the gallantry of the lifeboat crew during this rescue that she gave each a golden half sovereign.

The Llandudno lifeboat crew had a very busy spell in October 1872, when a northerly gale blew for several days along the North Wales coast. On 10 October *Sisters Memorial* was launched to the flat *Swallow*, of Runcorn, which was wrecked in very heavy seas in the bay, and saved her crew of three. The following day, the lifeboat went to the brigantine *Coila*, with the crew bringing a message ashore from her master requesting the assistance of a tug, which took the stranded vessel in tow. Then, on 16 October, as the storm raged on unabated, the lifeboat was launched to the flat *Peter*, of Liverpool, rescuing her four crew.

The last service undertaken with Hugh Jones as coxswain took place on the afternoon of New Year's Day 1875. The flat *Hester* had sailed from her home port of Conwy bound to Runcorn with a load of lead ore when she was seen in distress off Penmaenmawr in a fierce south-easterly gale. The lifeboat was launched at 2.30pm and it took five hours, requiring all the strength and energies of the whole crew, to weather the Orme and get to the casualty. Seas repeatedly broke into the lifeboat and filled her no fewer than four times during the outward passage. In spite of this, they were successful in taking off the two men from the *Hester* and landed the men at 9pm.

On the morning of 10 August 1885, *Sisters Memorial* was launched on a routine, quarterly exercise. A full south-westerly gale was blowing, with very rough seas. At about 10.30am the lifeboat crew spotted the small sailing boat *Mira*, with four men on board, in difficulties and flying a distress signal. The lifeboat immediately went to their assistance and rescued the four men but, as the lifeboat was returning to the shore, she was struck by a sudden, violent squall and capsized. The lifeboat quickly righted herself and all her crew, who were wearing their cork life-jackets, and three of the rescued men got back on board after she righted. But the fourth man from *Mira* was in danger of drowning, so lifeboatman John Roberts jumped into the sea and supported him until both were picked up by the lifeboat and brought ashore. The RNLI awarded the Thanks Inscribed on Vellum to John Roberts for his gallantry on this occasion. The RNLI's District Inspector Lieut Tipping RN subsequently held an inquiry into the events surrounding the capsize and reported that no blame was to be attached to anyone, while confidence in the lifeboat had been increased and the crew were indeed anxious to take her out again to practice at the first suitable opportunity.

Sisters Memorial was launched for what proved to be the last time on service at 2.40pm on 7 September 1887, going to the aid of the yacht *Haidee*, of Liverpool, which was sinking in rough seas and a strong north-easterly wind in the bay. While her two crew were taken being landed by another boat, the lifeboat managed to tow the yacht's tender ashore.

The establishment of the station had not been without its difficulties, and during the early years of its operation, its running was not altogether smooth. Maintenance and upkeep were something of a challenge for the crew, and on his first visit, in October 1861, the RNLI's District Inspector found the station to be 'in very indifferent order and the boat was dirty, the Coxswain not understanding his duties'. As for the boathouse, while the building itself was well built, the

floor was so badly laid that in parts it was a mass of stones and sand and this had damaged the carriage's wheels. In May 1862, as repairs to the floor had not been effected, the wheels themselves had to be replaced. However, by the following year, the floor had been relaid and the station was in better order.

In addition to problems with the boathouse, the boat itself was not always kept clean and this was noted on several of the Inspector's visits. In September 1876 it was reported that, 'the station was neither as clean nor as orderly as could be, and the crew were quarrelsome and discontented'. Two years later the lifeboat and gear were found to be dusty, as the doors of the boathouse had not been properly bolted, and the gear in the house was also untidy with 'the life-belts one on top of another'. It should be noted that there were no full-timers on the crew, and it seems unlikely that any guidance had been given as to how to maintain the lifeboat and station. However, in January 1880 it was reported to the RNLI that, 'the boat and house did not look as clean as they ought and, as the coxswain received £2 per annum extra salary, this was the more inexcusable'.

When the Inspector visited during this era, he did spend time resolving disputes, worked with members of the Branch to improve its functioning, and generally supported the station so that by the 1880s most of the problems had been overcome. However, one of the greatest difficulties was the provision of a sufficient number of horses to haul the boat to the beach and then launch it. On one occasion, when going to the assistance of the schooner *Water Lilly* which was aground by the Little Orme, as a result of the problem obtaining horses, the crew were badly delayed in getting away. Only four horses were available on this occasion, and the lifeboat arrived too late to give any help to the casualty.

Sunlight No.1

In 1887 the RNLI's Chief Inspector questioned the self-righting ability of the second *Sisters Memorial* lifeboat. As she was by then twenty years old, the RNLI decided to provide a new boat, fitted with 'all the latest improvements'. An order was placed with the RNLI's regular boatbuilder, Forrestt & Son of Limehouse, for a self-righter, 37ft in length and fitted with four water ballast tanks, pulling twelve oars, double banked. In July 1887 the new lifeboat satisfactorily passed her harbour trial. On 15 October 1887 she and her carriage were forwarded to North Wales, free of charge, via the London and North Western Railway, and they reached Llandudno a few days later. The old boat was then sold to the station's Honorary Secretary, George Felton, for £7, while the old carriage was sent to the RNLI's storeyard in London.

The new lifeboat was funded by Lever Bros, of Warrington, the famous soap manufacturers. The company had run a special Sunlight Competition to fund a new lifeboat, and eventually raised enough money to pay for two boats, the first of which, *Sunlight No.1*, came to Llandudno, while the second, *Sunlight No.2*, was stationed at Brighton in Sussex, both being of the same type. The names recognised a brand of soap that was then a household name, and the boats became well known at their respective stations.

The inauguration ceremony for the new lifeboat took place on 3 December 1887, and was a grand affair. The procession of lifeboat, crew and supporters started from the lifeboat house and proceeded through the town to the beach, where a platform had been erected for the ceremony. The Chairman of the local committee opened the proceedings, and as no representative from the donor was in attendance, the task of formally presenting the lifeboat

A depiction of Sunlight No.1, with her crew at the oars, possibly a publicity drawing produced for Lever Bros. (By courtesy of the RNLI)

was performed by the RNLI's District Inspector. A service of dedication was led by the Vicar, after which Mrs Crawley formally christened the boat *Sunlight No.1*.

After the ceremony, *Sunlight No.1* was duly launched for a short demonstration, watched by a large crowd, who turned out despite it being bitterly cold, with the crew being 'much pleased with her'. In the evening Mrs Jones Williams organised a dinner for the crew and other dignitaries. Sadly, Second Coxswain Edward Jones caught a severe cold during the day, and, a fortnight later, passed away. In consideration of his good service during the past twenty years, the RNLI helped towards his funeral expenses.

Sunlight No.1 served for fifteen years, during which time she saved twenty-six lives. She recorded her first service on 7 October 1889, being launched at 9.50am, under Coxswain Richard Jones, after two fishing smacks, *Perseverance* and *Ellen and John*, both from Hoylake, had signalled for assistance while they were at anchor three miles out in Llandudno Bay, as their anchors had started dragging. The lifeboat launched in heavy seas and a strong gale, reaching the casualties at 10.15am; she rescued four from *Perseverance* and landed them on the pier. She then went to the other smack and rescued her crew, landing them on the beach at 12.30pm.

By 1890 Llandudno had become a well-known seaside resort, being visited by many distinguished people taking their holidays. In September of that year the Queen of Romania spent some time in the resort and witnessed an exercise launch of the lifeboat and was so impressed that she made a £10 donation to RNLI funds.

A severe storm during the night of 6-7 November 1890 whipped up very heavy seas and, in the severe south-westerly gale, the schooner *Planet*, of Caernarfon, on passage from Runcorn to Plymouth, was caught out in the vicinity of Point Lynas. Unable to make any headway and forced to run before the wind, she was driven past Great Orme and into Llandudno Bay. The alarm was raised by a lighthouse keeper on the Orme, and *Sunlight No.1* was launched at 11.20am through a very heavy surf. After an exhausting pull at the oars, the crew succeeded in reaching *Planet* and taking five men off her, bringing them ashore. But no sooner had the crew rehoused the boat, than another call was received. A Norwegian barque was flying distress signals about seven miles north-east of the Orme's Head lighthouse. Unfortunately, as the lifeboat was being taken down to the beach again, one of the helpers, Robert Williams, while running alongside the boat, fell in front of one of the carriage wheels and was crushed to death.

When all was ready for the second launching, already delayed by this mishap, most of the crew refused to go out with the Coxswain in charge, claiming that he was not capable of taking command. This dispute, somewhat unusual in RNLI history, was the result of the crew's professed dissatisfaction with the Coxswain's handling of the boat on previous occasions, and the boat was then sent out with the Bowman in charge. Under his command, however, the men took their places without hesitation. After long and weary hours of searching in atrocious conditions without finding anything, the lifeboat returned with the crew cold, wet and

Below left: Lifeboat man Arthur Walley, who lost his life in August 1892 when he was tragically crushed under the wheels of the launching carriage. (By courtesy of the RNLI)

Below right: George J. Felton served as the station's Honorary Secretary from 1876 to 1890. (By courtesy of the RNLI)

A fine photograph of Sunlight N.o1 on her carriage, withe Tipping's plates on the wheels. Coxswain John Hughes and Second Coxswain John Williams are at the stern, so the photo can be dated to the early 1890s. The stocky man in the centre of the boat is almost certainly John Owen, Bronze medallist. (By courtesy of Llandudno RNLI)

thoroughly exhausted after a full day battling against the bitter elements. The barque was picked up the next day by a tug, with only her mizzen mast standing, and was towed into the Mersey. A fund was subsequently set up locally for the dependents of Robert Williams to which the RNLI contributed £100.

Launching the lifeboat was a dangerous business, and could also result in injuries being sustained by launchers. One shore helper, Henry Hughes, was run over by the launching carriage during a service launch on 7 October 1889, resulting in him breaking a leg. Fortunately, he survived, but he was in hospital for a month and was unable to work afterwards. The RNLI granted him £10 upon his discharge. This accident, and the deaths of Robert Williams, and Edward Jones before him in 1887, showed how dangerous lifeboat work could be. In fact, less than two years after the incident which saw Williams lose his life, there was another death. On 8 August 1892, as the lifeboat and carriage were being taken out on service, Arthur Whalley, one of the helpers, was run over by the carriage with fatal consequences.

In very rough seas and a westerly gale the barque *Eivion*, of Caernarfon, sought refuge in Llandudno Bay on the morning of 8 December 1893. Her crew dropped anchor, but when this failed to hold, a second anchor was let go. However, the strain of the two anchors was such that the ship's windlass smashed. Her crew immediately signalled for help, and *Sunlight No.1* was launched at 10.30am, proceeding under jib and reefed mainsail into the Bay. On the way out, the lifeboat was continually swamped by heavy seas, but managed to reach the casualty. At the request of the master, the

The third lifeboat to serve at Llandudno was Sunlight No.1, which was built at a cost of £529, and is pictured being launched from the beach, possibly for a lifeboat day. Horses were used to pull the lifeboat on her carriage from the boathouse. However, trouble rounding them up quickly enough from the Craig-y-Don end of town and the cost meant that, from 1899, about forty men were employed to pull the boat instead. All were given a tag so they could claim five shillings for their efforts. (By courtesy of Llandudno RNLI)

lifeboat returned ashore to organise the sending of a telegram asking for the tug assistance. A tug eventually towed the vessel to safety.

On 22 December 1894, a particularly stormy day in the north-west, lifeboats from twenty different stations were called out to a variety of incidents. *Sunlight No.1* was one of those called out, launching at 7.25am after flares had been fired from a vessel two miles north-east of the Orme's Head Lighthouse. She was the fishing ketch *Scotian*, of Hoylake, with a crew of four. It was a bitterly cold morning and the gale, which had blown all the night, was still increasing, but the crew toiled at the oars. Once on scene, the lifeboat crew made a rope fast, but the continual rolling of the ketch caused this to part several times, so the lifeboat sheered off. As a last resort, the Coxswain let go his anchor and by veering downwind came alongside. The ketch's crew of four were so numb from cold and exposure that it took the best part of an hour to get them aboard. This was not the end of their trials for they were forced to beat about for an hour or more, with heavy seas continually washing into the boat, before they reached the shore, where their arrival at 9.30am was greeted with cheers of relief by the waiting crowd.

What proved to be the last effective service performed by *Sunlight No.1* took place on 2 September 1897. In the morning, a schooner was seen ashore in Conwy Bay and the lifeboat, on her carriage, was taken to the West Shore at Llandudno and launched there at 9am. The casualty was *Dora*, of Chester, but her two crew got ashore safely in the ship's boat. Some of the lifeboat crew boarded the abandoned vessel and took her safely into Conwy.

The last Pulling and Sailing Lifeboats

At the turn of the century *Sunlight No.1* was due for replacement, but before deciding on a new lifeboat the Coxswain and the two of the most experienced members of the crew were sent by the RNLI to other stations in different parts of the country to choose the type of boat which they thought would be most suitable for Llandudno. This was common practice at the time, and enabled the crew to look at other boats then in service, and assess their merits. Following the visits, a standard self-righting type, 37ft in length and pulling twelve oars, was chosen. Such a boat was deemed powerful and large enough to cope with the seas around the Orme, yet not too heavy in view of the difficulties in launching by carriage over the beach.

The new lifeboat was built by Thames Ironworks, at Blackwall, the Thames-based boatyard used exclusively at this time, which built over 100 lifeboats. The cost of £908 was funded out of a

Above: A postcard showing Theodore Price being launched into the surf.

Below: With her crew ready with the oars, Theodore Price is prepared for launching off the North Shore, watched by a large crowd. (By courtesy of Llandudno RNLI)

legacy from the late Miss A.G.G. Rolleston, of Hyde Part Terrace, London, and the boat was named *Theodore Price*. She had her harbour trial on 2 June 1902, which proved satisfactory, and two weeks later she was sent to the station via the London & North Western Railway. Upon her arrival the old lifeboat was condemned and sold. A new set of horse launching poles was also sent, coming direct from the manufacturers in Bristol via the London & North Western Railway, although a new carriage was not provided, but the old one modified instead.

A new lifeboat house

Theodore Price was larger than her predecessor, and although she was housed in the existing boathouse upon her arrival, it was a tight squeeze. But by this time discussions were ongoing regarding the construction of a new boathouse. Indeed, since the mid-1890s discussions about a new boathouse had been ongoing as it was evident that not only was the old boathouse too small, it was also in an inconvenient position, sited next to the railway station.

In April 1897 the District Inspector discussed the possibility of obtaining a new site with Lord Mostyn, who 'promised to offer every facility for the Institution to dispose of the present site'. The London & North Western Railway Company were approached and their representative stated that he would recommend to his directors that they pay the Institution £200 for the ground on which the boathouse stood. With a buyer for the old house, the next step was to decide on the best site for a boathouse and the Inspector made three proposals: (1) a slipway 370 yards to low-water, or 470 yards to low water spring tides; (2) a shorter slip from the pier, which was objected to by the Pier company; and (3) a boathouse on piles next to the pier with a slipway, which would enable the boat to be launched at all states of the tide and from which a more powerful sailing boat could be operated.

Above: A fine photograph of Theodore Price on her carriage. (By courtesy of Llandudno RNLI)

Left: Theodore Price being hauled along the Promenade. (By courtesy of Llandudno RNLI)

Below: Theodore Price under oars in the Bay. (By courtesy of Llandudno RNLI)

The formal opening of the new boathouse in Lloyd Street, with crowds gathered to watch the ceremony, overseen by Lord and Lady Mostyn, with the latter declaring the building open. Lengthened and altered over the years, it served the station for well over a century, although launching the lifeboat from the West Shore became more difficult after the lower half of Lloyd Street was developed restricting access. (By courtesy of Llandudno RNLI)

The Deputy Chief Inspector discussed these three schemes with the local committee; the first was dismissed on account of cost, and the second because of the pier company's objections, leaving the third as the favoured option. Although it would be an expensive project, a boathouse and slipway would greatly reduce launch times, and the Deputy Chief Inspector was in favour of pursuing this plan. However, for some reason not specified in the RNLI's minute books, the Committee of Management decided that 'this scheme be not entertained and that the original recommendation (repairs to the house) be carried out'. It is probably that the cost – approximately £2,500 – was prohibitive, but understandably the local committee were very unhappy at the decision not to build the new boathouse.

By October 1897 repairs to the boathouse had been carried out, but they were only temporary. The RNLI Chief Inspector was pursuing another option, recommending that 'a boathouse of an ornamental character be erected on a site to be obtained from the Lord Mostyn'. Matters moved slowly, however, and in May 1898 Lord Mostyn declined to provide the site that had been selected by the Chief Inspector, leaving the local committee 'much disappointed at this failure'.

The silver lock on the door of the new lifeboat house in Lloyd Street, opened by Lady Augusta Mostyn in 1904, was presented to her after the ceremony. (Lord Mostyn)

More than two years passed before further steps were taken to resolve the situation. On 5 June 1900 the Deputy Chief Inspector and District Inspector visited a site in Lloyd Street which Lord Mostyn was willing to let for a nominal rent of five shillings. It was deemed suitable but not until the following year were plans drawn up for the boathouse that would be built here. Meanwhile, in July 1901 the Deputy Chief Inspector visited the station and found both lifeboat and house 'in a very untidy condition'. No doubt morale at the station was low due to the failure to provide a new boathouse and the unsuitability of the existing building.

However, just as a resolution to the situation seemed to have been found, another dispute occurred between the national and local committees. In September 1901 the designs for the proposed new boathouse, which would cost £1,025, were forwarded to Llandudno by the RNLI's Architect. But when presented to the local committee at a meeting in October 1901, they were deemed unsuitable as there was no provision for 'a club room for the men', or living accommodation for a caretaker. The local committee unanimously disapproved of the designs and stated that 'the lifeboat work in Llandudno cannot be adequately carried out without a room being provided for the men to meet and receive instructions'. In addition, Lord Mostyn's offer of the site to the RNLI was on condition that the boathouse had the desired crew accommodation, but had the RNLI's Deputy Chief Inspector known that such conditions were attached to the offer, he would not have recommended its acceptance.

At this point, negotiations broke down, and the RNLI withdrew their plans, ascertaining in November 1901 whether the present house could be enlarged for a new and larger boat. This was opposed by the local committee, who believed it was, 'unwise to make the old lifeboat house serve, as space was so limited as to be a danger to those engaged with the lifeboat'. In June 1902 the new lifeboat arrived, as described above, but in September 1902

Crowds watch from the beach as Theodore Price is put through her paces for lifeboat day. (By courtesy of Llandudno RNLI)

With her sails raised,
Theodore Price is launched
off her carriage and into
the surf. She was fitted with
two lug sails and a jib, had
two water ballast tanks and
two sliding drop keels. (By
courtesy of Llandudno RNLI)

the District Inspector found her and the boathouse 'in a dirty and untidy state'. The local committee were very unhappy about the failure of the RNLI to provide a new boathouse, and feelings were running high in the town, with the District Council prepared to stop the usual street collections.

This impasse lasted several more months until, in June 1903, negotiations reopened for the site offered by Lord Mostyn for the new boathouse. The solicitors for Lord Mostyn were preparing the lease, and in July 1903 the RNLI's corporate seal was fixed to an agreement to lease the site. In September 1903 the RNLI's Architect had obtained tenders for the construction work, and the estimate of £1,254 10s 0d from Henry Hughes was accepted. The house took less than a year to erect, and on 12 May 1904 the RNLI's Architect reported that it had been completed, with the work 'carried out in a very satisfactory manner'. The site in Lloyd Street was in a more central part of the town, an ideal location for enabling the lifeboat to be launched from either shore, and the total cost was £1,370 16s 1d.

Opening the new lifeboat house

The formal opening of the new lifeboat house took place on 9 June 1904, with the *Llandudno Advertiser* newspaper reporting the event under the headline 'A memorable day at Llandudno'. Not only was the new lifeboat house opened, but so was a new Post Office, and there was a silver wedding presentation to Lord and Lady Mostyn. The opening of the new boathouse was the third ceremony of the day, with Lady Mostyn formally declaring

A fine photograph of Theodore Price under oars off the pier. (By courtesy of Llandudno RNLI)

the building open in the presence of a crowd 'which must have numbered some thousands of persons'. A platform had been erected in front of the building for the dignitaries, led by Lord and Lady Mostyn, with the RNLI represented by Lieut Rowley RN. The Rev J. Raymond, the station's Honorary Secretary, read a statement giving the background to the building's construction:

'For several years the local committee had sought to secure a better house in a better position, and Lord Mostyn had been most zealous in working for this object. At length the London Committee consented to erect a new house, which cost about £1,500, upon a site generously given for that purpose by Lord Mostyn, the President of the Local Committee. Everything had been done to make it up-to-date in all that tended to secure efficiency at the station. Ample space, manifold fittings for gear,

Theodore Price is rowed away from the beach and out into the Bay. (By courtesy of Llandudno RNLI)

and simplicity of mechanism in doors, gates, etc, offered every facility for speedy response when the call for a service came. The boat was one of the newest type of self righting boat, having two drop keels... The crew, thirteen in number, had every confidence in the capabilities of the boat, and would therefore the more cheerfully respond when called upon to serve.' Following the speech, Lord Mostyn said: 'I have to ask my wife to open the door of the boathouse', and Lady Mostyn used a silver key to open a silver lock, formally opening the boathouse.

Despite the positive words spoken during the ceremony about the enthusiasm of the crew, the District Inspector's report of the launch of the lifeboat that followed the formalities was stated that 'the Coxswain had no control over his crew, half of whom were the worse for liquor on this occasion.' However, this appears to have been an isolated incident and in March 1905, at his next report, the District Inspector reported that 'everything was working smoothly'

Twenty-eight years of service

Although the years surrounding her arrival had been challenging for those involved with the station, in twenty-eight years of service *Theodore Price* was to prove her worth, for in that time the crew had nothing but praise for her seaworthy qualities. She launched forty-two times on service, going out to various vessels, but mostly helping the schooners that dominated coastal cargo transportation during this era. A few local fishing boats were also assisted, with the lifeboat acquitting herself well throughout.

The first service performed by *Theodore Price* took place on 1 February 1903, after the keepers on the Orme's Head lighthouse had sent word that a steamer was in distress six miles north-east of the lighthouse. The lifeboat put out at 9.50am, getting away within eighteen and a half minutes of the rockets being fired to alert the

A postcard showing Theodore Price in heavy seas in the Bay, titled 'For those in peril on the sea'. (By courtesy of the RNLI)

Left: Theodore Price on the beach watched by a large crowd, possibly for lifeboat day. (By courtesy of Llandudno RNLI)

Below: Theodore Price probably being recovered onto her carriage, as just one crewman is in the boat while the others assist from the beach. (By courtesy of Llandudno RNLI)

Lifeboat crew on board
Theodore Price. The two
in peaked caps are almost
certainly Robin Williams
(Second Coxswain), standing,
and John Owen (Coxswain),
seated. (By courtesy of
Llandudno RNLI)

crew, a 'performance that reflects the very highest praise on all concerned', according to the local newspaper account. Although it was a Sunday morning, a large crowd had assembled on the Promenade to watch the launch, with the lifeboat getting away safely, finding the 503-ton steamer *Wylam*, of Limerick, bound for her home port with a general cargo. The previous evening, in rough seas and gale-force winds, her cargo had shifted and she had a serious list, taking in water which was 8ft deep in her engine room by the time the lifeboat arrived. *Theodore Price* stood by as the vessel slowly made her way into Llandudno Bay, where she dropped anchor, with the lifeboat bringing the pilot, Mr Bibby of Liverpool, ashore. The weather later moderated and, eventually, the steamer was able to get under way again.

At 4pm on 12 February 1904 the keepers on the Orme's Head lighthouse reported a schooner in distress three miles to the north-west. *Theodore Price* was launched at 4.24pm and headed out into very rough seas and a severe south-westerly gale. The casualty was *Progress*, of Wicklow, carrying coal. Two steamers were standing by, and the lifeboat crew found that the schooner's four crew had been taken aboard one of the steamers, which was bound for Llanddulas. So some of the lifeboat crew boarded the schooner and succeeded in beaching her safely at Abergele, with the lifeboat closely escorting her all the way. Coxswain Hughes then turned back towards Llandudno, and with the lifeboat heading into the gale heavy seas repeatedly swept clean over the boat. Slowly, they made their way back, but not until nearly 5am the next day was the lifeboat safely beached at Llandudno, having been at sea for over twelve hours in truly appalling conditions.

Theodore Price on her carriage in the town sometime in the 1920s. Coxswain John Owen can be picked out on the boat with his Bronze medal awarded in 1919. (By courtesy of Llandudno RNLI)

Theodore Price on her carriage on the Promenade; Coxswain John Owen (third from left), blowing his whistle. Almost all the crew are wearing newly supplied kapok life-jackets. (By courtesy of Llandudno RNLI)

While the smack *Midsummer*, of Douglas, was lying at anchor in the bay, on the evening of 2 September 1907, the wind unexpectedly changed direction and increased in strength, until a north-westerly gale was blowing, churning up very heavy seas. The smack began to drag her anchor and so the skipper, who was on board on his own, hoisted a distress signal. The town was filled with holidaymakers at the time and thousands lined the Promenade to watch as *Theodore Price* was launched at 8pm. The skipper was quickly rescued by the lifeboat and, to the cheers of the large crowd watching the rescue, safely brought ashore.

A casualty close to Llandudno occurred on 8 January 1908 in which *Theodore Price* played a small part. The schooner *William and Henry*, on passage from the Dee with rock salt for Wicklow, was forced to take shelter close to the pier in the lee of the Orme. She had been buffeted by strong winds all morning, causing the hull to leak and, as water was quickly coming in, beyond the capacity of the pumps, signals were displayed asking for help. Before *Theodore Price* could get to the schooner, however, a boat reached the vessel and took off her three-man crew. Later, some men went back on board the schooner and, by double manning the pumps, kept her afloat until the weather changed and she could be removed for repairs.

A month later, in February 1908, the crew underwent one of their most severe trials when the lifeboat was launched on a wild rainy morning, with the weather soon becoming gale-force. The ketch *Lily Garton*, bound for Caernarfon, was in distress on the Conwy side of the Great Orme. As the lifeboat made her way round the Great Orme, although sailing well, she encountered extremely heavy seas that broke aboard, causing some damage made worse when the centre-plate jammed. While the crew were trying to release this, the lifeboat was swamped by a heavy breaking sea which knocked one of the crew, Evan Evans, who was already suffering badly from exposure, against the gunwale, leaving him unconscious. In spite of the crew's seamanship and their repeated efforts, the partly disabled lifeboat could make no headway against the wind. The coxswain could now do nothing to help the ketch and had no alternative but to beach the lifeboat to save her and the crew. Although Evans recovered, conditions had been so bad that day that another member of the crew, John Williams, died shortly afterwards due to the severe exposure he suffered on this occasion. He left a widow and three young children, the RNLI, contributing £100 to a fund set up for them.

Between 1908 and the end of the First World War, further services were mostly to fishing craft. On the evening of 6 July 1910 *Theodore Price* saved two from the smack *Hero*, of Rhyl, and on 30 October 1911 assisted the schooner *Jane and Ann*, of Caernarfon, bound for Fishguard with coal and caught out in a north-westerly gale. Six lifeboat crew members went on board, helped to raise the anchors and get the vessel under way again. The local fishing boat *Primrose*, with a crew of two, was blown out to sea on the evening of 18 October 1912, but the lifeboat crew could not find the boat in the dark. They continued searching until 12.30am, and then returned ashore to get a hot meal and change of clothing. The lifeboat set out again just before dawn and, at 7am, found the missing boat a mile and a half off Little Orme. Ten lives were saved on 10 August 1914 when two local pleasure boats, *Dylis* and *Annie*, were caught in a sudden squall. *Theodore Price* had been on a routine exercise when the boats got into difficulty and so was already at sea.

Medal-winning service

One of the most dramatic rescues in the station's history took place on 27 March 1919. The schooner *Ada Mary*, on a voyage from Ireland to Hoylake with timber, was caught in a fierce north-westerly gale which destroyed her sails. She drifted before the wind and tide towards

Penrhyn Bay, west of Colwyn Bay. The crew of two managed to let her anchors go, but by the morning these were failing to hold so a message was sent to Llandudno for the lifeboat and *Theodore Price* was launched at 1pm. As the lifeboat battled her way round to the casualty, she was repeatedly swept by huge seas, being completely swamped at least three times, the lifeboat crew only preventing themselves from being washed overboard by hanging on to the lifelines. But, eventually, they reached the schooner and Coxswain Owen skilfully manoeuvred the lifeboat alongside, so that the two exhausted men could be rescued. But getting back to Llandudno proved particularly difficult as *Theodore Price* could make little or no headway beating against the westerly gale and tide, and after several hours the crew were forced to give up the attempt, so Coxswain Owen decided to beach the lifeboat at Colwyn Bay, which he did

Theodore Price ready to be hauled off her carriage. Note the Tipping plates on the wheels, fitted to stop the wheels from sinking into the sand. The man in the tie may be the Honorary Secretary or an RNLI Inspector who was accompanying the boat to sea for what was probably an exercise launch. (By courtesy of Llandudno RNLI)

Left: Theodore Price and her crew, wearing their kapok life-jackets, outside the lifeboat house in Lloyd Street. (By courtesy of Llandudno RNLI)

Below: Many hands haul on the ropes to get Theodore Price to the promenade.

Sarah Jane Turner, with sails set, is launched into the surf off the North Shore in February 1931. She was fitted with one large lug sail, a mizzen and a jib. (By courtesy of Llandudno RNLI)

Opposite top: Matthew Simpson being hauled along Lloyd Street on the way to the Promenade. (By courtesy of the RNLI)

Opposite bottom: Matthew Simpson under sail off Llandudno. (By courtesy of Llandudno RNLI)

and the two men were landed. For this skilful service under the most arduous conditions, Coxswain John Owen was awarded the Bronze medal by the RNLI.

Services during the 1920s were largely routine in nature, with two in 1920 to the same schooner, *Dundaig*, of Padstow. She was sheltering in Llandudno Bay on 8 January 1920 during a strong gale when her crew of five were taken off for safety by *Theodore Price*. They were later taken back when the gale abated, but had to be rescued again three days later during another gale. That same day she had also gone to the schooner *Jane and Ann*, of Caernarfon, in difficulty, and landed her crew of four. In December 1922 *Theodore Price* helped a local rowing boat, and on 29 October 1923 saved the fishing boat *Alice* and two drifting boats.

Theodore Price was launched for what proved to be the last time on service on 22 October 1927. During that afternoon the motor yacht *Delphore*, of Liverpool, arrived off Llandudno and her crew, three in number, dropped anchor near the Pier. But early that evening the wind began to increase and the yacht dragged her anchor, drifting beneath the Pier. *Theodore Price* was launched at 8pm and rescued the three people from the casualty, which later went ashore on the rocks. The rescue was witnessed by Tom Stone, who recalled the incident, writing in 1995:

'I watched the launch, which in those days was impressive as the boat was propelled by sheer manpower . . . Running around to the side of the pier, we saw the lifeboat come round the pierhead under sail and make a pass along the wreck and saw *Delphore*'s crew jump into it. Considering the sea that was running, the Coxswain did a fantastic job as he had to make a ninety-degree turn to port within a very short distance to avoid the pier and make for open water.'

Reserve lifeboats for three years

Theodore Price was withdrawn from service in June 1930, and was replaced by another 37ft self-righting lifeboat, *Sarah Jane Turner*, which had been built in 1901 for Montrose and served there until 1924, when she was placed in the Reserve Fleet. *Theodore Price* was sold locally and converted into a cabin cruiser, named *Maralic*, and in private ownership was twice in trouble herself, in the Conwy estuary and later in the Mersey. In fact, the first service launch at Llandudno by *Sarah Jane Turner* was to *Maralic*, on 4 October 1930. The lifeboat put out to her assistance at 12.15pm, but the cabin cruiser was able to return to Conwy without assistance and the lifeboat returned to station at 4.45pm.

On 29 March 1931 *Sarah Jane Turner* went to help the yacht *Bluebell*, which was in difficulties in the Conwy Estuary, but, as with *Maralic*, the yacht got out of trouble unaided. The only effective service to be performed by *Sarah Jane Turner* at Llandudno took place on 18 July 1931. She launched at 7.15am to the aid of the yacht *Frosette*, of Liverpool, which had two people on board. The lifeboat escorted the yacht to Rhyl and returned to Llandudno at 8pm after a long day at sea for her volunteer crew.

On 27 July 1931, just over a week after this service, *Sarah Jane Turner* was replaced by another 37ft self-righting lifeboat, pending the arrival of a new motor lifeboat at the station. This second temporary boat, *Matthew Simpson*, had been built in 1903 for the Berwick station in Northumberland, where she served until 1924. She then spent four years at Ramsey on the Isle of Man before coming to North Wales. *Matthew Simpson* was launched only once on service at Llandudno, on 29 July 1933, after an aeroplane was reported to have crashed into the sea. However, despite a thorough search by the lifeboat crew nothing was found. And so ended the pulling and sailing era at Llandudno, which lasted more than seventy years and saw more than 100 lives being saved.

Matthew Simpson at Berwick-upon-Tweed. Built in 1903, she served the Northumberland station for twenty-one years, during which time she saved sixty lives. She was sold out of RNLI service in September 1933.

Motor Lifeboats come to Llandudno

The end of the pulling and sailing era at Llandudno came in 1933 after two reserve self-righters had served while the station's new motor lifeboat was under construction. Although the RNLI's first powered lifeboats saw service during the early 1900s, more than two decades passed before a suitable design of motor lifeboat was available for stations where carriage launching was employed, such as Llandudno. The first motor lifeboats were too large to be launched from a carriage, and so were either kept afloat or launched down a slipway. At nearby Beaumaris on Anglesey a motor lifeboat had been provided in 1914, the 43ft Watson type *Frederick Kitchen*, one of the first purpose-built motor lifeboats to see service. She was launched down a slipway from a newly-built boathouse, a set-up that had been considered for Llandudno in the 1890s but never adopted.

Llandudno's first motor lifeboat was the 35ft 6in self-righter Thomas and Annie Wade Richards, which had a single engine and carried auxiliary sails in case of engine break down. (By courtesy of the RNLI)

Llandudno required a carriage-launched motor boat, but, not until the 1920s had engines been developed with a power-to-weight ratio suitable for fitting into lifeboats that were small and light enough to be manhandled on a beach and launched from a carriage. The First World War had delayed motor lifeboat development, but during the inter-war era several advances were made, including the use of twin engines and the development of carriage-launched boats. The first carriage-launched motor boats entered service in the 1920s, and by the 1930s they were being built in sufficient numbers for more or less all the old pulling and sailing lifeboats to be replaced in the RNLI's fleet.

Two carriage-launched designs were introduced: the motor self-righter in 1929 and the Liverpool class a year later, both of which were 35ft 6in in length and single-engined. The Liverpool was not self-righting but had a greater beam, while the self-righter was in many ways similar to the pulling and sailing lifeboats that had served Llandudno hitherto, with a narrow beam and high end boxes that gave her a righting capability in the event of a capsize. The first of the new self-righting type entered service at Hythe in Kent in 1929, and between then and the outbreak of the Second World War twenty-one boats of the class were built. Llandudno's boat was one of the last. She was one of three to be completed during 1933 by the well-known boatyard of J. Samuel White at Cowes, at a cost of £3,010 0s 7d.

She measured 35ft 6in in length with a beam of 9ft 3in, weighed six and three-quarter tons and was powered by a single 35hp six-cylinder Weyburn AE6 engine, which was housed in a cuddy amidships in a watertight compartment. The engine itself was watertight and would continue running even if the engine room were flooded. She carried enough fuel to give her a radius of action of forty-seven nautical miles at her maximum speed of 7.13 knots, with the engine developing 832rpm. At her cruising speed of six and a half knots, with the engine developing 710rpm, the radius of action increased to sixty nautical miles.

The hull was divided into six watertight compartments and had 115 air cases. She carried a crew of seven, and could take thirty people on board in rough weather. *The Lifeboat* of November 1934 stated: 'If a sea breaks on board she can free herself in twelve seconds, and if she were capsized, even with a hole in her bottom, she could right herself in four seconds'. She was more advanced than any lifeboat that had served the station hitherto, and was welcomed to Llandudno on 18 September 1933. She had left Southampton on board the steamer *Lancashire Coast* on Friday 15 September, and arrived in Liverpool two days later. On Monday 18 September the boat was handed over to Coxswain Robin Williams,

Second Coxswain Trevor Davies, Bowman Goulding, Mechanic James Jones and the RNLI's District Engineer Dorkings, and they left Liverpool at 10am, arriving in Llandudno at 3pm, making nine knots during the passage. The new boat was provided out of two legacies, one from Dr Thomas Wade Richards, of Llangadock, and one from Miss Sarah Lewis, of Aberystwyth. Dr Richards' legacy had also helped to fund the motor lifeboat *G.W.* at Moelfre, which was built in 1930.

Naming ceremony

Her formal naming ceremony took place just over a year later, on 28 September 1934, with the *Llandudno Advertiser* carrying a full page report on the proceedings, stating that 'Glorious sunshine favoured the official launch of Llandudno's new motor lifeboat'. Presiding over the occasion was Lord Mostyn, President of the Llandudno Branch of the RNLI, and the grandson of Lady Augusta Mostyn, who had christened the first Llandudno Lifeboat in 1861. Between its opening and the ceremony, the station's lifeboats had rescued 114 lives. Among those taking part in the ceremony were Lord Mostyn, Sir Godfrey Baring, chairman of the RNLI, and Mr G.A. Humphreys, Chairman of the Branch, as well as all the station officials. Also present were William Jones, of Llandudno, and Richard Thomas, of Conwy, who had attended the launch of the first Llandudno lifeboat seventy-three years previously.

The scene during the naming ceremony of Thomas and Annie Wade Richards at Llandudno on 28 September 1934, with hundreds of supporters in attendance. (By courtesy of Llandudno RNLI)

On board Thomas and Annie Wade Richards for her naming ceremony are Robin Williams, Jim Jones, John Williams, David Lloyd-Jones, Trevor Davies, Tommy Davies, Dai Jones and Bill Goulding. (By courtesy of Llandudno RNLI)

Hundreds of people in attendance at the naming ceremony of Thomas and Annie Wade Richards on 28 September 1934.

Miss A.E. Lewis, cousin of Miss Sarah Lewis, one of the two donors, presented the lifeboat to the RNLI, and she was received by Sir Godfrey Baring, who expressed the gratitude of the Institution to the two donors. He then formally presented the lifeboat to the station and she was received by Mr Humphreys. After a Service of Dedication conducted by the Rector of Llandudno, the Rev Canon T.J. Rowlands, assisted by the Rev W.H. Compton and the Rev H. Harris Hughes, the boat was christened *Thomas and Annie Wade Richards* by Miss Lewis, with the crowds cheering.

A vote of thanks to Lord Mostyn, Sir Godfrey Baring, and Miss Lewis was proposed by Thomas J. Jones, chairman of the Llandudno Urban District Council, and seconded by the Hon Mrs H. Lloyd Mostyn. In his speech, Mr Jones said he could assure Miss Lewis that, 'the munificent gift of the late Dr Thomas Richards and the late Miss Sarah Lewis, her cousin would be zealously cared for, capably manned with a crew ever-ready to run all the risks in answer to the call of duty'. After the singing of Hen Wlad Fy

Watched by crowds of supporters and well-wishers, Thomas and Annie Wade Richards is launched at the end of her naming ceremony. (By courtesy of Llandudno RNLI)

Nhadau (the Welsh national anthem) and the National Anthem, the lifeboat was launched. When she returned ashore, the crew were presented with woollen helmet-scarves, a gift from Mrs E. Manby, of Codsall, Staffordshire. And thus, with the good wishes of the whole town, *Thomas and Annie Wade Richards* started her work of life-saving on the North Wales coast.

Thomas and Annie Wade Richards served Llandudno for two decades, during which time she launched fifty-seven times on services and saved thirty-eight lives. The casualties were very

Thomas and Annie Wade Richards being launched in front of large crowds, probably for lifeboat day. (By courtesy of Llandudno RNLI)

The first tractor to serve Llandudno was T14, a Clayton & Shuttleworth type which had been built in 1925. It was sent to help with launching and recovering the motor lifeboat, and had served at Port Logan until that station was closed in 1932. The vehicle remained at Llandudno until 1946. (By courtesy of Llandudno RNLI)

Thomas and Annie Wade Richards outside the boathouse. The fourth crew member from the left is James Jones, the station's first Mechanic, and far right is Coxswain Robin Williams, son of John Williams, who retired as Second Coxswain of Theodore Price in 1904 after having completed forty-three years of service. (By courtesy of Llandudno RNLI)

varied during this period, with yachts, fishing boats and dinghies all assisted, along with lightvessels and a submarine, and the following descriptions cover a selection of the rescues undertaken by the Llandudno crew in their first motor lifeboat.

The new boat had undertaken two services before her naming ceremony, the first on 6 May 1934. The yacht *Mizpah*, of Liverpool, had lost her sails in heavy seas and a southerly gale, two miles off the Little Orme. The lifeboat launched at 11am in torrential rain, saved the three crew, who were totally exhausted, and towed the yacht to Conwy. By coincidence, the next service launch was to the same yacht, which was dragging her anchor in Llandudno Bay in heavy seas and a near gale on the morning of 20 August 1934. The lifeboat launched at 10.30am, saved the three people on board and again towed the yacht to safety.

On the afternoon of 18 October 1935 she launched at 3.40pm to the fishing boat *Barbara*, whose three crew were totally exhausted from constant baling. The boat was being carried out to sea by a stormy offshore wind, so the three men were rescued and their boat was towed back to shore at 4.35pm. On 7 August 1936 the lifeboat went to the yacht *Mona*, of Heswall, which had dropped anchor in a dangerous position in Llandudno Bay and was caught in a strong north-easterly wind during the evening of 6 August. *Thomas and Annie Wade Richards* put out at 1.30am in very rough seas, took three people off the yacht and landed them at Conwy.

A fine photograph of the Thomas and Annie Wade Richards outside the boathouse in Lloyd Street, probably in the early 1930s showing her carriage to good effect. The men in peaked hats are, left to right, Robin Williams (Coxswain), Trevor Davies (2nd Coxswain), and James Jones (Motor Mechanic). (By courtesy of Llandudno RNLI)

Submarine Thetis sinks in Liverpool Bay

In June 1939 a maritime disaster took place in Liverpool Bay, fifteen miles north of the Great Orme, and made headline news. The newly-launched submarine *Thetis* left her builders' yard at Birkenhead on 31 June for dive trials. Aboard were fifty-three officers and men, together with fifty other personnel, including naval officers, Admiralty overseers, employees of the builders and contractors, a Mersey pilot and two caterers. At 1.35pm *Thetis* made her first dive, but from this she failed to rise. This was later found to be due to water entering one of the forward torpedo tubes and flooding the forward compartment. The attending tug, *Grebecock*, became anxious when the submarine had not resurfaced, sent a message to Liverpool, and a full scale operation was organised to try and locate the sunken *Thetis*. At 7.30am the next day the destroyer *Brazen* found part of the after end of the

submarine above water, but all attempts to raise it higher failed. Four of the trapped men escaped through an escape hatch, but at 3pm the exposed part of the submarine slid below the surface, and the ninety-nine men still on board lost their lives.

Thomas and Annie Wade Richards played only a minor part in this essentially naval operation, taking Dr Madoc-Jones, the station's Honorary Medical Advisor out to the destroyer *Somali* on the morning of 22 June, and then standing by, before returning to Llandudno at 10.30pm. Initial attempts at raising the submarine failed but, after the war broke out and the need for all types of vessels became urgent, *Thetis* was raised in a difficult salvage operation. She was towed and beached at Traeth Bychan, near Moelfre, where the

bodies of the entombed men were recovered and taken for burial at Holyhead. After temporary repairs the submarine was towed back to her builders at Birkenhead where she was refitted. Renamed *Thunderbolt*, she served in the Mediterranean with distinction until she was sunk by enemy action off Sicily in 1943.

During the Second World War, lifeboats answered many calls to aircraft, British or German, that had crashed in the sea as well as other casualties of the war. However, calls were largely routine and casualties were not in trouble due to enemy action. On the night of 28 January 1940 *Thomas and Annie Wade Richards* stood by the 4,772-gross-ton cargo ship *Gleneden* in freezing conditions. The ship was on her way from Saigon to Liverpool with a cargo of maize and joined a convoy at Gibraltar. The convoy divided in the western approaches, with a small group of ships, including *Gleneden*, making their way to Liverpool. Zig-zagging relatively close inshore to avoid U boats, *Gleneden* struck Carreg Hen, a rocky shoal a few miles south of South Stack lighthouse on Anglesey. Left to her own devices by the rest of the convoy and escorts, and leaking badly, the ship was deliberately grounded off Dutchman's Bank, near Beaumaris, on the east coast of Anglesey after her captain realised his vessel would not reach Liverpool.

The entire crew of sixty were evacuated by Moelfre lifeboat, in two trips, during the night of 29-30 January and landed at Beaumaris. Holyhead lifeboat was also launched and made a record passage to reach the ship, a feat of true seamanship, but arrived just

A fine photograph of Thomas and Annie Wade Richards launching from the beach, watched by a good crowd. There is relative shelter in the bay, but a gale is evident beyond the Orme's Head. (By courtesy of Llandudno RNLI)

Above and opposite: Thomas and Annie Wade Richards paying a courtesy visit to Conwy in 1951, mooring at the quay beneath the castle. (By courtesy of the RNLI)

as Moelfre lifeboat had taken off the last of the crew. Although some of *Gleneden's* cargo was salvaged, the ship could not and she broke up when she lay eventually disappearing into the sand. Although not strictly speaking a casualty of war, the *Gleneden's* loss was certainly due to the exigencies of war.

During the morning of 9 November 1940 the trawler *Leonard*, of Fleetwood, tied up alongside the pier with her holds full of water in a north-westerly gale with heavy seas. A pump was obtained from the Auxiliary Fire Brigade, but, as it could not be worked from the pier, the pump and several firemen, were put aboard *Thomas and Annie Wade Richards*, which was launched at 11.30am. While the pump was put to work, some of the lifeboat crew helped unload the trawler's cargo of fish and some of her gear. The work went on throughout the day and night, until 6.45am on 10 November. Once most of the water had been pumped out, the boat then set off for Bangor, escorted by the lifeboat, which returned to her boathouse at 1pm, over twenty-five hours after being launched.

Thomas and Annie Wade Richards was launched at 5.05pm on 27 January 1943 to help the local fishing boat *Pilot No.3*, which

A fine photograph of Thomas and Annie Wade Richards being pulled through the town by tractor T14 (reg no. XW 2075), which served from 1933 to 1946. (By courtesy of Llandudno RNLI)

had broken down two miles east of the pier. In rough seas and a southerly gale, the disabled boat was found to be waterlogged and so the crew of three were saved and their boat taken in tow. As they headed back, the lifeboat crew found another fishing boat, *Eira*, in difficulties in the heavy seas. Her crew of three were also rescued and their boat taken in tow.

The Mersey Docks and Harbour Board boat, used to supply the various lightvessels in the area, was unable to take food to the Western Lightvessel, moored fifteen miles north-west of Orme's Head, due to a fierce south-westerly gale in January 1944. So, at the request of the Harbour Board, *Thomas and Annie Wade Richards* was launched at 10.30am on 7 January to take the supplies to the lightvessel, whose crew had been without food for three days. A Letter of Thanks was sent to the station by the Mersey Docks and Harbour Board thanking the crew for their help on this occasion.

Post-war services

Three effective services were performed by *Thomas and Annie Wade Richards* during 1946. On 30 July 1946 she saved two men who had put out from Rhos-on-Sea in a small boat to go fishing off Colwyn Bay, but been caught out in rough seas. On 29 August 1946 she went to the fishing boat *Delia*, which had broken down and was leaking, in rough seas and a near gale-force wind off Rhos-on-Sea. The crew of two were rescued and their boat towed

Case LA type launching tractor T40 and the launching carriage at the top of the slipway awaiting the return of the lifeboat. T40 served Llandudno from 1948 to 1956. (By courtesy of Amy Haywood Francis)

ashore at Colwyn Bay. On the afternoon of 27 September 1946 she went to two rubber dinghies which were drifting out to sea off Colwyn Bay, saving two men and landing them at Llandudno.

On the afternoon of 21 January 1947, while the Western lightvessel was being towed to another location, the wire tow line parted, and one of the crew of the lightvessel was injured. *Thomas and Annie Wade Richards* was launched at 4pm with a doctor on board to help. The lifeboat crew reached the lightvessel sixteen miles north of the Great Orme and the doctor went aboard. He treated the injured man and was then brought back to Llandudno by the lifeboat, which beached at 11.45pm.

When the converted fishing vessel *The Witch*, was seen drifting three miles off Abergele in very heavy seas and a north-westerly

Recovery of Thomas and Annie Wade Richards on the beach in 1951, towards the end of her time at the station. (By courtesy of the RNLI)

Thomas and Annie Wade Richards afloat off Llandudno. Wreaths are being laid so this could possibly be at the site of the loss of HM Submarine Thetis, where a memorial service was conducted on 7 June 1939, a few days after the submarine had been lost. The Chairman of Llandudno Council, as well as the station's Honorary Secretary, J.E. Hallmark, were in the boat for this occasion. After leaving Llandudno in February 1953, she was sold out of service a month later to a Criccieth owner and used as a fishing vessel there and at Aberystwyth and Rhyl. She was later moved to Coburgh Marina, Liverpool, but was broken up around 2003. (By courtesy of Llandudno RNLI)

gale on the morning of 15 November 1947, *Thomas and Annie Wade Richards* was launched to help. The lifeboat crew found the owner, his wife and their two young children, plus two young men, on board the converted boat, whose engines had broken down. As it proved impossible for the lifeboat to tow the casualty in the prevailing conditions, the owner, his wife and their two children, were rescued, albeit with some difficult. However, the two young men refused to leave, so the lifeboat returned to Llandudno, landing the rescued people at 2.30pm. Later that afternoon *The Witch* drifted close to the shore, the two men jumped overboard and swam ashore, the boat later becoming a total wreck at Abergele.

What proved to be the last effective service by *Thomas and Annie Wade Richards* at Llandudno took place on 1 April 1952. She was launched at 3.36pm after a fishing boat had been reported to be in difficulties two miles off the Great Orme. The vessel, *Liver Bird*, of Conwy, had one man and his dog on board. The man had badly injured a finger, so he was taken aboard the lifeboat and given first aid. His boat was then towed to Conwy and the lifeboat returned to Llandudno at 9.15pm.

Post-war lifeboats

B y the 1950s *Thomas and Annie Wade Richards* was reaching the twentieth year of her service and, powered by a single engine, was seen as relatively outdated. Twin-engined motor lifeboats were the norm and so, in February 1953, another lifeboat, *Tillie Morrison, Sheffield*, was sent to the station. This was a 35ft 6in self-righter, similar to the boat she replaced, but was powered by two 18bhp Weyburn AE4 petrol engines. She had been built in 1947 for Bridlington but, while on service there on 19 August 1952, capsized, which resulted in one of her crew losing his life. As a result she was replaced at Bridlington and, after a major overhaul, was reallocated to Llandudno. On 18 February 1953 *Thomas and Annie Wade Richards* was taken to Gallows Point boatyard at Beaumaris with *Tillie Morrison, Sheffield* arriving by road that evening. At the same time Councillor H. Neville, newly on the local committee, asked the Council to provide night lighting on the promenade for the station's night operations.

The 1947-built Tillie Morrison, Sheffield, on display on the promenade, with collecting boxes nearby. She served at Bridlington for five years before coming to Llandudno. (By courtesy of Llandudno RNLI)

Tillie Morrison, Sheffield on the Promenade. (By courtesy of Llandudno RNLI)

Tillie Morrison, Sheffield served at Llandudno for just over six years, saving eight lives. Her first effective service took place on 1 June 1953 when she was launched at 12.40am to the aid of a pinnace from HMS *Verulam*. The pinnace had dropped anchor in Llandudno Bay after her rudder had broken and the lifeboat towed the boat to safety. Twelve people were landed and the lifeboat returned to the boathouse at 4.15am. Towards the end of the year, on 13 December 1953, a fishing competition was held in Llandudno Bay involving numerous small boats. But when the weather began to deteriorate the boats had to return to shore. However, two failed to come back so at 3.40pm *Tillie Morrison, Sheffield* launched, with a local motor boat also putting out to help. The lifeboat then escorted all three boats safely ashore.

Tillie Morrison, Sheffield on the Promenade, with a viewing platform drawn up alongside. The boat was regularly brought down to the Promenade for display. (By courtesy of the RNLI)

In rough seas and a near gale-force south-westerly wind, the fishing boat *Anna Rosa*, of Rhyl, broke down off Llandudno on the afternoon of 23 October 1954. She was taken in tow by the fishing boat *Ever Ready*, of Conwy, but, as the towline had parted, *Tillie Morrison, Sheffield* was launched. She reached the two fishing boats when they were two miles north-east of the Orme's Head lighthouse, by when the tow line had been reconnected. The lifeboat escorted the two boats as they headed towards Conwy and,

Tillie Morrison, Sheffield, grounding on the North Shore slipway with skids laid in readiness for her recovery. The member of shore crew at the bow is wearing a working suit, cloth cap and shoes, and trying not to get wet. (By courtesy of Llandudno RNLI)

Tillie Morrison, Sheffield being recovered on the promenade in 1953. When the boat arrived at Llandudno, a catwalk was provided in the boathouse so that visitors could view the boat, and the boathouse floor was resurfaced. (By courtesy of Llandudno RNLI)

when off the lighthouse, the fishing boat *Pendorfa* arrived on scene and attempted to take over the tow. But *Anna Rosa* began drifting towards the rocks, the lifeboat standing by until the towline had been secured. She then escorted all three boats safely to Conwy, and returned to station at 9.30pm having been out for five hours.

About 11am on 7 September 1957 Harry Wilman, the borough engineer and surveyor of Colwyn Bay, was in his office when he was informed that a boat was in distress in the bay. He got a message to the Llandudno lifeboat and then, with one of his clerks, Leslie Hill, fetched his 12ft aluminium dinghy and outboard motor from his home and took it to the beach. A south-westerly gale was blowing, and beyond the pier the sea was very rough. The boat in trouble was a 12ft wooden dinghy, with two young men and two girls in, who were unable to row back to the beach against the strong wind. So Wilman and Hill immediately launched their aluminium dinghy and started the motor. They threw a line to the wooden dinghy which, at the second attempt, was made fast and the towing began. The wooden dinghy was half full of water by this stage, and was difficult to steer. As they headed towards the shore, the wooden dinghy suddenly sank and the four young people were thrown into the water. Hill cut the tow rope, but at that moment the outboard engine failed.

Annie Ronald and Isabella Forrest being launched on service 17 June 1961 to rescue a man and boy missing in rough seas off Rhos of Sea. (By courtesy of Llandudno RNLI)

Wilman and Hill tried to row back to the four young people, who were in the water, and with some difficulty restarted the engine, the plugs of which were wet, but then saw one boy throw up his hands just before going under. They picked up one of the girls at the first attempt and a quarter of an hour later rescued the second. They continued to look for the boy until the engine ran out of petrol. Meanwhile, *Tillie Morrison, Sheffield* had been launched, putting out at 11.35am. She reached the dinghy and took the two men and the two girls on board and then carried out a search for the boys. No trace of them was found, unfortunately, and so the four survivors were landed at Colwyn Bay. The lifeboat crew made a further search for the missing youths, but without success, and so they returned to station at 2.15pm. For this service the Thanks of the Institution Inscribed on Vellum were accorded to Harry Wilman and Leslie Hill.

Annie Ronald and Isabella Forrest

In April 1959 *Tillie Morrison, Sheffield* was taken to Beaumaris to be overhauled and in her place came a non-self-righting 35ft 6in Liverpool class boat, *Annie Ronald and Isabella Forrest*, which had been built in 1936 for St Abbs. Although she was fitted with a single 35hp Weyburn AE6 petrol engine, as opposed to the twin engines of *Tillie Morrison, Sheffield,* the crew preferred her and in June 1959 she was permanently reallocated to Llandudno, with *Tillie Morrison, Sheffield* being withdrawn from service. She was sold by the RNLI in November 1959 and, after being converted into a fishing boat, ended up on the Tyne at Newcastle, where she remained for many years.

In November 1959 a new launching carriage was supplied to the station to that there would be, according to the *Llandudno and District Advertiser*, 'swifter launchings'. The new carriage had automatic release gear which meant there was no need for a second shore helper on the tractor. The new carriage replaced one

The lifeboat crew in 1961 with Annie Ronald and Isabella Forrest, with her official number (O.N.792) written on her stern as she was officially a Reserve lifeboat rather then the station boat. Pictured are, left to right: Gordon Bellamy (Coxswain), Ernest Lloyd Jones (Second Coxswain), Harold Griffith (Bowman), Caradoc Harris (Mechanic), Chris Jones, Mike Haywood, Harold Haywood (Shore Signals) and Tom Griffith (Second Tractor Driver); kneeling at front are Dennis Heritage (Head Launcher), Colin Watson, Oakley Kelly (Second Mechanic), Eirian Williams and Jack Jones (Tractor Driver). (By courtesy of the RNLI)

built from steel and timber, parts of which were sixty years old. The RNLI's Naval Architect, Richard Oakley, who designed the 37ft Oakley class, supervised the trials of the new carriage.

Annie Ronald and Isabella Forrest was allocated to the station on a temporary basis while a decision was made as to future cover. In December 1961 the RNLI Inspector, Cdr Hill, attended a meeting of the local committee and stated that, some years previously, the RNLI had wanted to close the station and only his representations had stopped this. However, he explained that the station would receive a new boat and tractor in the near future. In the meantime, *Annie Ronald and Isabella Forrest* continued to serve, and during her five years at the station she saved a very creditable twenty-one lives, with her services much in demand.

Her first effective service at Llandudno took place on 4 October 1959, when she put out at 12.06pm, with Second Coxswain Samuel Lloyd-Jones in command, after a rowing boat, with four men on board, got into difficulties off the Great Orme in choppy seas and a strong southerly wind. The lifeboat rescued the four men and towed their boat, and the men, back to the beach, within half an hour of launching. The lifeboat was called out again that afternoon, at 1.46pm, again with the Second Coxswain in command, to the aid of a small boat, which was in difficulties three miles off Penmaenmawr. The casualty was the speedboat *Aires*, with two men on board and they were rescued and put ashore, together

Annie Ronald and Isabella Forrest outside the lifeboat house with her sail raised. (John Lawson Reay)

with their boat, at Penmaenmawr. The Coastguard then radioed the lifeboat crew reporting that a small yacht was believed to be in difficulties in the area, but although the crew made a thorough search, no yacht in need of assistance was found and the lifeboat returned to station, beaching at 4.40pm.

After a report had been received that a dinghy, with a doctor and his son on board, was drifting out to sea off Rhos-on-Sea on the evening of 17 June 1961, *Annie Ronald and Isabella Forrest* was launched at 7.20pm. In rapidly deteriorating conditions, with rough seas and a near gale force wind, the lifeboat crew searched a wide area without success. The search was called off for the night, as visibility fell to less than fifty yards in the inky blackness, and

Annie Ronald and Isabella Forrest on the promenade, with a viewing platform in place for visitors to look on board. (From an old postcard supplied by Nicholas Leach)

THE LIFEBOAT, LLANDUDNO

Above: Annie Ronald and Isabella Forrest at sea in the early 1960s. (John Lawson-Reay)

Below: Annie Ronald and Isabella Forrest being launched at North Shore using tractor T31 (registraton number FGU 821), which served from 1956 to 1961, having been built in 1938. On the stern of the lifeboat are the words 'Reserve Lifeboat O.N.792'. (By courtesy of Llandudno RNLI)

Gordon Bellamy was appointed Coxswain in January 1961 and stayed in the post for ten years. (By courtesy of the RNLI)

Annie Ronald and Isabella Forrest towing the fishing boat Christina, of Rhyl, on 22 June 1963; the boat and its five occupants were brought to safety. (By courtesy of the RNLI)

A fine photograph of the single-engined 35ft 6in Liverpool motor Annie Ronald and Isabella Forrest on the Promenade. (Jeff Morris)

Annie Ronald and Isabella Forrest returns to Llandudno after saving two people from a small boat on 4 October 1959. (Jeff Morris)

The Case L tractor T31 towing Annie Ronald and Isabella Forrest on her carriage across the beach after a second service launch on 4 October 1959. (Jeff Morris)

the lifeboat returning to Llandudno Bay at 11.45pm, where she was moored. Her crew came ashore for a change of clothing and a rest, and put to sea again at 3am, being joined in the search by HMS *Belton*. The minesweeper eventually found the missing dinghy and rescued the doctor and his son. The two survivors were transferred to the lifeboat and landed at Rhos, with the lifeboat returning to station at 6.20am after a long and difficult night for the volunteers.

In 1961 the station celebrated its centenary and, on Sunday 5 July, a service of thanksgiving was held at Holy Trinity Church. It was conducted by the Venerable Archdeacon Gwynfryn Richards. During this Service, the Deputy Chairman of the RNLI, the Hon Valentine Wyndham-Quin, presented a Centenary Vellum to Honorary Secretary Thomas Taylor, who handed it to Coxswain Bellamy for safe keeping.

Annie Ronald and Isabella Forrest launching on exercise, 25 May 1961. (Jeff Morris)

Annie Ronald and Isabella Forrest launching off her carriage, early 1960s. (John Lawson Reay)

Annie Ronald and Isabella Forrest being launched on service on 7 January 1962. (By courtesy of the RNLI)

In rapidly worsening conditions on 9 August 1962 *Annie Ronald and Isabella Forrest* was launched at 2pm after the yacht *Hazard*, with three adults, a child and a dog on board, got into difficulties off the Conwy Estuary. The motor boat *Alice* put out from Conwy to help and got a line aboard the disabled yacht, keeping the craft's head-to-sea until the lifeboat arrived. The lifeboat then took *Hazard* in tow, back to Conwy, as well as escorting the motor boat *Alice*. The lifeboat eventually returned to her station at 5.45pm.

After the Coastguard reported that a motor boat, with six small yachts in tow, appeared to be making little headway in choppy seas and a near gale-force south-easterly wind, on 14 August 1962 *Annie Ronald and Isabella Forrest* was launched at 1.30pm. She reached the motor boat at 2.20pm and took her and the six yachts in tow to Deganwy, then returning to station at 8.40pm. As she was being recovered on the beach, the police reported that a man was trapped by the incoming tide on rocks at the foot of the Little Orme. So the lifeboat was launched again, towing a small rowing boat to the scene. This was manned by two of the lifeboat crew, who rescued the man from the cliffs and transferred him to the lifeboat, which finally returned to station at 10.10pm.

In the early hours of 14 April 1963 the Beaumaris and Llandudno lifeboats were called out to search for a cabin cruiser, reported to be broken down. At the time, the reserve lifeboat *Frank and William Oates*, another single-engined 35ft 6in Liverpool class boat, was on

temporary duty and she was launched at 2.45am. At 8am the coaster *Southern Coast* radioed that she had found the cabin cruiser nine miles north of the Great Orme, and the reserve lifeboat went to the reported position. The three people on board the cabin cruiser were transferred from coaster to lifeboat, which towed the boat to safety and landed the three survivors at Llandudno at 10.30am.

What proved to be the last effective service performed by *Annie Ronald and Isabella Forrest* at Llandudno took place on 7 September 1963. She launched at 1.45pm after a small yacht was reported in difficulties off Orme's Head lighthouse. The lifeboat had been about to launch on exercise to go to Colwyn Bay for an RAF

Annie Ronald and Isabella Forrest towing the fishing boat Christina, of Rhyl, into Conwy on 22 June 1963. The lifeboat had launched at 1.29pm in a fresh south-westerly wind and found the fishing boat with five people on board and a broken down engine. The lifeboat returned to her station at 5.15pm. (John Lawson Reay)

Annie Ronald and Isabella Forrest being brought back into the boathouse in Lloyd Street in the early 1960s. After spending five years at Llandudno, she was sold out of RNLI service in July 1965 having had a life-saving career of almost thirty years. (By courtesy of Llandudno RNLI)

Wing's Day display and, as it was learned that the yacht, which had two men on board, had been trying to get to Rhos-on-Sea, the lifeboat towed it there and then continued on to Colwyn Bay, arriving at 3pm. But, forty-five minutes later the Coastguard called Coxswain Bellamy on the radio to inform him that a yacht was in difficulties off Rhos. The lifeboat made for the new location, and found the same yacht in trouble again, so the lifeboat towed it ashore. The lifeboat was then called to the assistance of a Yacht Club guard boat, which had gone to the aid of a capsized yacht, and stood by while the righted yacht was towed to the shore. The lifeboat eventually got back to her station at 7.30pm.

Annie Ronald and Isabella Forrest being launched. (By courtesy of Llandudno RNLI)

Lilly Wainwright

O n 2 February 1964 a new lifeboat arrived at Llandudno, having been sailed from the Groves and Guttridge boatyard at Cowes where she had been built. Named *Lilly Wainwright*, she was one of the new Oakley class boats designed by and named after the RNLI's Consulting Naval Architect, Richard Oakley. The design was 37ft in length, had a beam of 11ft 6in, and was manned by a crew of seven or eight. Developed during the mid-1950s, it was the first lifeboat design to have a high degree of inherent stability and also self-right in the event of a capsize. Self-righting was achieved through an ingenious water ballast system which transferred 1.54 tons of water ballast into a righting tank on the port side to right the boat in the event of a capsize. Previous self-righters, such as *Tillie Morrison, Sheffield*, had a narrow beam, needed to enable them to self-right, but were thus less stable. This relative lack of stability made them less popular with some crews, who preferred a broader-beamed boat.

The 37ft Oakley class lifeboat Lilly Wainwright on trials in 1964 shortly after being completed. (By courtesy of the RNLI)

The new 37ft Oakley Lilly Wainwright after completion at Groves & Guttridge boatyard in Cowes, January 1964. She was yard number G&G 605 and was one of four Oakleys built at the Groves & Guttridge yard in the early 1960s. (By courtesy of the RNLI)

During self-righting trials of the 37ft Oakleys, it took about six seconds for the boat to return to the upright from the overturned position. The boat's hull was constructed of wood and, with a displacement of 12.4 tons, it was suitable for handling ashore and carriage launching over a beach. Power came from twin Ford Parsons Porbeagle four-cylinder diesels of 52bhp, which gave a maximum speed of about eight knots. On trials, *Lilly Wainwright* achieved a maximum of 8.18 knots, consuming 4.43 gallons of diesel per hour which gave her a radius of action of eighty–eight nautical miles. At her cruising speed of seven knots the radius of action increased to 170 nautical miles with a fuel consumption of just under two gallons an hour.

The new 37ft Oakley Lilly Wainwright arrives at Llandudno for the first time, early February 1964. (By courtesy of Llandudno RNLI)

HRH Princess Marina, Duchess of Kent, at the naming ceremony of Lilly Wainwright. Chairman Harold Neville escorted the Duchess, accompanied by Capt the Hon Wyndham-Quinn (left above). She was presented with a bouquet of flowers (above) and met the volunteer crew (left). (By courtesy of the RNLI)

In total twenty-six Oakleys were built, with that allocated to Llandudno, official number 976, being the ninth. She was ordered on 15 June 1962 from Groves & Guttridge and construction took about eighteen months. The new lifeboat reached Llandudno after a passage from her builder on the Isle of Wight. The passage crew was made up of Gordon Bellamy (Coxswain), Caradoc Harris (Mechanic), Christmas Jones and Bob Jones, and they were accompanied by the RNLI's District Inspector Harold Harvey and District Engineer D. MacMillan. R.D. Pike, the Assistant District Inspector, was on board for the last part of the passage.

The naming ceremony of the new lifeboat, which cost £32,230 11s 6d, took place on 15 May 1964. The boat had been provided out of a legacy from Mr J.H. Wainwright, of York, plus a gift from the Arthur Jowett Fund, provided by the late Arthur Jowett, of

Batley, Yorkshire, as well as RNLI funds. Councillor H. Neville, chairman of the Llandudno branch, opened proceedings, and Captain the Hon V.M. Wyndham-Quin, Chairman of the RNLI's Committee of Management, formally handed the lifeboat to the branch, being accepted by Mr T. Taylor, honorary secretary.

After a service of dedication conducted by the Bishop of Bangor, the Rt Rev G. Williams, HRH Princess Marina, Duchess of Kent, President of the RNLI, christened the new lifeboat *Lilly Wainwright*. Princess Marina had arrived by a helicopter of the Queen's Flight, landing on a cricket ground only two minutes drive from the promenade. Among the official guests was Lady Mostyn, President of the Llandudno Ladies Lifeboat Guild, whose husband's grandmother who had christened the first lifeboat at Llandudno in 1861. Once the formalities were over, the new lifeboat was launched to a chorus of hooters from the Beaumaris lifeboat, which was in attendance, and local pleasure craft.

Before her naming ceremony, *Lilly Wainwright* had been called out for her first service, launching at 4.05pm on 13 March 1964 after a man in a sailing dinghy had been carried out to sea off the Conwy Estuary on an ebb tide. A helicopter eventually spotted the dinghy on rocks at Orme's Head, and some of the lifeboat's shore-helpers climbed down to investigate. The dinghy was found jammed between the rocks with no sign of her occupant, and it

The volunteer crew on board Lilly Wainwright on 15 May 1964 for her naming ceremony, with local children also supporting the event. The new Case 1000 launching tractor, T73, was sent to Llandudno, for launching and recovering th new 37ft Oakley lifeboat. (By courtesy of the RNLI)

The scene on the Promenade during the naming ceremony of Lilly Wainwright on 15 May 1964, with hundreds of people in attendance. (By courtesy of the RNLI)

Crowds attending at the naming ceremony of Lilly Wainwright. (By courtesy of the RNLI)

Lilly Wainwright being recovered after the demonstration launch at the end of her naming ceremony on 15 May 1964. (By courtesy of the RNLI)

was assumed, after a search of the area, that the man had got ashore safely. The dinghy was refloated and rowed out to the waiting lifeboat by one of the shore helpers, and the lifeboat towed the dinghy back to the beach at 6pm.

For more than twenty-five years *Lilly Wainwright* served as Llandudno's lifeboat, during which time she is credited with launching 116 times and saving fifty-eight lives. Her rescues were routine rather than spectacular, and the following descriptions encompass those that are representative of the rescue work she undertook with her volunteer crew. At 6.34pm on 3 May 1964, less than two weeks before her naming ceremony, she was launched to help the motor yacht *Almeria*, with a crew of four, which was in difficulties in Conwy Bay. The yacht was found anchored in

Lilly Wainwright on the promenade, with steps for viewing the boat adjacent. (By courtesy of the RNLI)

two fathoms of water with heavy seas, whipped up by a westerly gale, breaking over her. One of the lifeboat crew was put aboard and secured a tow line. The anchor was slipped and the yacht was towed to Conwy. As she was being moored, the lifeboat crew learned that there was a sick woman on board so they brought a doctor from Conwy to attend to her and then took the Doctor back to the Quay. The lifeboat returned to station at 10.43pm.

After the keepers at the Orme's Head lighthouse had reported a small yacht capsized 400 yards off the light on 16 April 1965, *Lilly Wainwright* was launched at 1.20pm. In choppy seas and a stiff north-westerly wind, she reached the casualty, *Wiz*, of Penmaenmawr, crewed by three people. They had succeeded in righting the dinghy and climbed back on board, but were soaking wet and exhausted. So they were taken on board the lifeboat, given first aid and brought ashore, together with their dinghy, at 3pm.

Inshore lifeboats come to Llandudno

A few days after this service, one of the RNLI's new high-speed inshore rescue boats (IRB) was sent to Llandudno. The first IRBs had been brought into service at Aberystwyth in May 1963 and during the 1960s the small fast craft were sent to many more stations, often being co-located with the slower offshore lifeboats, such as at Llandudno. IRBs were 15ft 6in in length, built of neoprene-proofed nylon and driven by a 40hp outboard engine, which gave them a top speed of over twenty knots. Manned by a crew of two or three and capable of being launched within minutes, they proved to be ideal for dealing with incidents involving small yachts, cabin cruisers, bathers, people cut off by the tide and other such incidents.

The first inshore rescue boat at Llandudno. No.54, Mechanic Caradoc Harris is wearing in the white cap Harris, and the man at the helm is Meurig Davies. (By courtesy of the RNLI)

Lilly Wainwright's first 'splash launch' on 15 February 1964. When there was sufficient water at Llandudno's North Shore slipway, typically two hours either side of high water, Lilly Wainwright was launched using this method. The boat was positioned at the top of the slipway with the tractor and, with the rear trailer wheels locked straight, the whole carriage and boat were let go, moving down the slipway at increasing speed. A rope was attached to the end of the trailer so that it could be recovered up the slipway. The retaining chains had to be let go at precisely the right moment. Only the aft quarter chains were securing the boat to the carriage at this point.

The first IRB which came to Llandudno, No. 54, was called out for the first time on service on 23 May 1965 saving a youth after he had become trapped on some rocks. Further services were undertaken during the summer, and on the evening of 5 September 1965 IRB No. 54 launched to help a yacht capsized off the Conwy Estuary. The yacht's two crew were picked up and put ashore at Deganwy. The following summer IRB No. 54 continued to prove an asset to the station, launching at 7.05pm on 9 June 1966, to the aid of the motor launch Puffin, which had broken down off the West Shore. The disabled boat, which had a crew of three, was towed to Conwy and the ILB was beached at Deganwy, where she was recovered onto her launching trolley and taken back to her boathouse by road. Less than three weeks later, the IRB was again in action, launching at 6.12pm to save two girls who were cut off by the tide on a sandbank off the West Shore.

In October 1966 a new inshore lifeboat, No. 109, was sent to Llandudno. She cost approximately £1,000 with all her gear and was presented to the RNLI, by two local sisters, Mrs S.J. Sutcliffe and Miss M.A. Law, of Roumania Crescent, in memory of Mrs Sutcliffe's husband. On the evening of 11 October 1966 they watched the new IRB being launched off the North Shore, along with Mr C. Neville (Branch Chairman), Gordon Bellamy, Mrs J. Wilkes (Chairman of the Ladies Guild), Mrs Cave Rogers (Secretary of the Guild), and Cdr Harold Harvey (RNLI District Inspector). Two days later trials with the new boat were undertaken,

Lilly Wainwright puts to sea shortly after she had arrived on station. When built, Lilly Wainwright had an open aft cockpit, was not fitted with radar and her engine casing was light grey. (By courtesy of the RNLI)

carried out by Mechanic Caradoc Harris and Second Coxswain Meurig Davies. IRB No.109, which was later redesignated D-109, served at Llandudno until October 1976.

The new inshore boat undertook several services during her first season. She was launched at 6.45pm on 30 May 1967 after a boy fell over cliffs on the Great Orme. The injured boy was rescued and, together with a member of the local Mountain Rescue Team, was brought ashore. The ILB then returned to the rocks and brought off seven other people who had been helping. On 29 June

The reserve 35ft 6in Liverpool motor Lucy Lavers coming ashore in 1967. Built in 1940, she served at Aldeburgh as the No.2 lifeboat until 1959, after which she spent another nine years as a Reserve lifeboat. During her stint at Llandudno she was not called upon to undertake any rescues. (By courtesy of Landudno RNLI)

Above: The first inshore rescue boat in North Wales came to Llandudno in 1965. The boat, No.54, cost £750 and is pictured coming ashore with Second Coxswain Meurig Davies and Honorary Secretary Thomas Taylor in the boat. Jumping out is crew member Gordon Short. The small fast boat soon proved her worth.

This photograph appeared in the Llandudno Advertiser of 6 May 1966 and relates to an incident on Saturday 30 April 1966 in which the first IRB, No.54, was involved. The newspaper report explains what happened:
'Four Liverpool boys trapped by the tide at the foot of the Little Orme were saved through the bravery of a fifth boy [Alan Walker] who made a 150 yards 'life or death' swim to organise a rescue. Bruised and gashed, he crawled up the beach after rounding the headland and told a holiday maker who alerted Llandudno Lifeboat crew. Using the Inshore Rescue Boat, Caradoc Harris, the lifeboat mechanic, rescued the other boys, Vincent Coleman, Peter Keating, Frank Bell and Peter Tyson, all aged thirteen. Alan's bravery was praised by Mr Harris particularly as the earlier unsuccessful attempt to swim for help by Peter Tyson had failed'. (John Lawson Reay)

Members of Llandudno Lifeboat Youth Guild in the 1960s; pictured are Vivienne Shepherd, David Sargent, Lady Mostyn, Caradoc Harris (Mechanic) Robin Willliams (pier master), Marcus Elliott (now LOM) and Hilary Neville, circa 1969. (By courtesy of Llandudno RNLI)

1967, after red flares had been fired by the three crew on board the dinghy *Sea Imp* two miles off Llandudno, No. 109 put out to rescue the three people and towed the dinghy ashore.

Meanwhile, *Lilly Wainwright* continued to be called on for the more difficult services and, on 8 December 1967, she was called out in a storm. In extremely heavy seas and a fierce north-westerly gale, with frequent heavy snow-showers, the motor vessel *Farringay*, of Cardiff, developed engine trouble in Liverpool Bay, so the New Brighton lifeboat was called out. She got a line aboard the disabled vessel, but was unable to prevent her from drifting towards Orme's Head. *Lilly Wainwright* was therefore launched to help, but still the vessel continued to drift before the storm. The Rhyl lifeboat was the next to be launched and, with her help, the drift was halted, a tug eventually reaching the disabled vessel and taking her in tow.

Late on the afternoon of 26 March 1968, after the crew of the fishing vessel *CO359* had been seen firing red flares off the Great

The second inshore rescue boat, and the first one to serve the station in the long term, is formally presented on Sunday 11 October 1966. Pictured are, left to right, Mrs S.J.Sutcliffe (one of the donors), unknown, Miss L.A. Law (one of the donors), Councillor Harold Neville, Caradoc Harris (Mechanic), Gordon Bellamy (Coxswain), Thomas Taylor (Honorary Secretary) and Meurig Davies (Second Coxswain). (John Lawson Reay)

Two photographs showing the inshore lifeboat No.109 being brought ashore after a service call. (By courtesy of the RNLI)

Orme, *Lilly Wainwright* was launched. She put out at 4.45pm into very choppy seas and a near gale force south-westerly wind. The lifeboat found a disabled motor launch with two men on board, and with a punt in tow. The men were rescued and told the lifeboat crew that their fishing boat had been towing the launch and the punt, but had then struck something in the water and sunk, forcing the two men to scramble aboard the launch. The motor launch and the punt were towed back to Llandudno, where the men were landed.

At 4.15pm on 6 May 1968 *Lilly Wainwright* and her crew were called out to the cabin cruiser *Calypso*, with five people on board, which had broken down a mile west of the Orme's Head lighthouse. In rough seas and a full westerly gale, the cabin cruiser was towed to Conwy, which was reached at 5.45pm. As the lifeboat was rounding the Great Orme on her way back to her station, the Coastguard asked the lifeboat crew to go to the assistance of the motor vessel *St Trillo*, which had fouled one of her propellers a mile and a half north of Llandudno. She had 450 American tourists on board and was taking them back to the 26,000-ton cruise liner *Kungsholm*, which was anchored off Llandudno, after the Americans had been on a tour of North Wales. Coxswain Bellamy was asked to take some of the passengers off *St Trillo* and

Lilly Wainwright at Llandudno was a popular subject for postcard publishers. The three postcards reproduced here show the boat in her early years at the station, during the 1960s and 1970s, when her engine casing was painted grey. She is seen being recovered on the beach (top); on display on the promenade with the tractor (middle), probably Fowler type number T56 (on station 1969 to 1977); and being launched down the slipway at the North Shore (bottom), using Case 1000D tractor T72 (on station 1965 to 1969), dressed overall, possibly for the annual lifeboat day.

Lily Wainwright outside the lifeboat house on 18 May 1968 and on display on the Promenade, 28 May 1968. Her engine casing is painted grey and she has not had the operational number, 37-09, added. (Jeff Morris)

Inshore Rescue Boat No.54 on the Promenade on 28 May 1968. (Jeff Morris)

secured alongside. But in the rough seas, *St Trillo* was rolling heavily and, as most of the passengers were elderly, it was decided to wait until further help arrived. Lifeboats from Rhyl, Beaumaris and Moelfre were all called out and the large trawler *Kilravock* put to sea from Conwy. Her crew succeeded in getting a line aboard *St Trillo*, with the skipper, Jack Williams MBE, displaying superb seamanship manoeuvring *St Trillo* alongside the pier. Lifeboats from Llandudno, Rhyl and Beaumaris stood by as the motor vessel was towed to the pier, where the passengers were disembarked. *Lilly Wainwright* continued to stand by while divers freed the motor vessel's propeller, and the lifeboat eventually returned to station just after 2am, after a very long call for her volunteers.

During 1969 the IRB No.109 undertook a series of routine rescues. It was launched at 4.30pm on 7 May 1969 to a trimaran with two adults and two children on board, which had dragged her anchor and been driven under the Pier. The ILB towed the trimaran to safety. As the ILB was being recovered at 5pm, she was called out again, this time to an inflatable dinghy with eight men on board in difficulties off the Orme's Head lighthouse. Just over two weeks later, on the evening of 24 May 1969, IRB No.109 rescued a boy, who had fallen 70ft into the sea over cliffs near the Orme's Head Lighthouse. He was rushed ashore and an ambulance took him to hospital.

On 21 September 1969 both Llandudno lifeboats were called into action after squally weather caused several sailing dinghies to capsize off the Little Orme while they were racing. The Yacht Club's rescue boats went to help and at 1pm IRB No.109 was launched, with *Lilly Wainwright* following five minutes later. In rough seas and a very strong offshore wind, the lifeboat rescued two men and took their dinghy in tow, and another three abandoned dinghies were also towed in. Meanwhile, the IRB had towed two other dinghies in and they were all beached at Llandudno.

Lily Wainwright being recovered on the beach in the 1960s. (By courtesy of Llandudno RNLI)

Above: David Lawson Reay, son of shore helper John Lawson Reay, at the wheel of Lilly Wainwright, with Coxswain Gordon Bellamy, in the late 1960s.

Right: On board Lilly Wainwright are, left to right, Bob Jones, Caradoc Harris (Mechanic), Chris Jones (Bowman) and Gordon Bellamy (Coxswain). (By courtesy of Llandudno RNLI)

On 20 June 1971 *Lilly Wainwright* was launched into rough seas and her crew faced a north-westerly gale. Red flares had been sighted two miles off Llandudno at 9am, and the lifeboat was called out to investigate. The casualty, the cutter *Sea Foam*, had two people on board and the engine had broken down, so a tow line was secured and the disabled boat was towed into Llandudno Bay. As the boat's crew of two were suffering badly from exhaustion, the inshore lifeboat D-109 was launched at 10.40am to bring them ashore while their boat was put on a safe mooring. *Lilly Wainwright* returned to station at 12.05pm.

Thanks on Vellum service

On the afternoon of 27 April 1974 the Llandudno volunteer crew carried out a very fine service. After a report had been received that a sailing dinghy had capsized off the Little Orme, the crew of the ILB were summoned. A force five north-easterly wind was whipping up rough seas as, at 3.30pm, an attempt was made to launch D-109. But as the ILB was floated, she was picked up by heavy surf and thrown back onto the beach. At 3.35pm a second attempt was made to launch and this time she got away safely, manned by Mechanic Robert Jones as Helmsman, and crew members Gordon Short and Hugh Hughes. The sailing dinghy was found on the rocks with one of its occupants nearby and the other, who had tried to climb up the cliffs, stranded 30ft above sea level. Using his boathandling skills, Helmsman Jones took the ILB in between the rocks on the back of a large wave, to rescue the first man, after which the ILB was brought clear and taken back out to sea again. During this operation the engine was damaged.

Coxswain Meurig Davies with Dic Evans, the well-known retired medal-winning Coxswain from Moelfre. (By courtesy of Llandudno RNLI)

Helmsman Jones was concerned for the wellbeing of the rescued man, who was suffering from exposure, and as the other man was safe for the time being, Helmsman Jones decided to take the ILB ashore, and landed the survivor at 4.35pm. The local Mountain Rescue Team was called out to rescue the other man from the cliff face and, as the outboard engine on the ILB had been damaged, the Rhyl ILB was called to provide help. The man on the cliff was lowered into the Rhyl ILB by the Mountain Rescue Team and then brought ashore at Llandudno. For this fine service the RNLI accorded the Thanks Inscribed on Vellum to Helmsman Robert Jones. Vellum service certificates were presented to crew members Gordon Short and Hugh Hughes.

In May 1974 *Lilly Wainwright* was sent away for a routine overhaul, and in her place came the relief 37ft Oakley class lifeboat *Vincent Nesfield* on temporary duty. *Vincent Nesfield* had undertaken a relief duty at Llandudno from February to July 1970, but had not been called out. During her second spell, however, which lasted until December 1974, she answered three calls. The first came

Crew aboard Lilly Wainwright in the boathouse: John Roberts, Chris Jones (Second Coxswain), Ken Lathom, Gordon Short, Meurig Davies (Coxswain), Hughie Hughes. Glyn Jones, Bob Jones (Mechanic), in the early 1970s. (By courtesy of Llandudno RNLI)

Mechanic Bob Jones, helmsman of D-109 in April 1974, with his Thanks Inscribed on Vellum, flanked by his crew, Gordon Short and Hughie Hughes. (By courtesy of Llandudno RNLI)

during the afternoon of 26 June, when she went to the aid of a speedboat which was in difficulties off Colwyn Bay in very rough seas and an easterly gale. The crew of two on board the casualty, *Tee Jay*, had dropped anchor and were taken aboard the lifeboat and brought ashore. On 30 September 1974 *Vincent Nesfield* searched for a speedboat which had been reported missing during the evening. The boat was found anchored off Penmaen Head, her crew having gone ashore in a dinghy to get fuel; once they were back on board their boat, the lifeboat escorted it to Rhos. The final service by the relief lifeboat took place on 6 November 1974, when she helped the fishing boat *Untouchable*, of Conwy, which was disabled, with a crew of three on board, and so was towed to Conwy. Lilly Wainwright returned to Llandudno on 2 December 1974 and *Vincent Nesfield* left to take up her next relief duty at Ramsey on the Isle of Man.

In February 1977 a new inshore lifeboat, D-250, was sent to Llandudno. She had been provided out of funds donated to the RNLI by Tesco Stores Ltd and, on 12 July 1971, the new boat was formally handed over. The handing over ceremony took place on the Promenade and was performed by Harold Quinton, Managing Director (North West) of Tesco and the ILB was received on behalf of the RNLI by Mrs T.W.E. Corrigan, of Anglesey, representing the RNLI's Central Appeals Committee. Mrs Corrigan handed the boat for safe keeping to Honorary Secretary Thomas Taylor. A brief description of the boat was given by Lt Cdr George Cooper, RNR, District Inspector, North West. The formal dedication was led by the Rector of Llandudno, the Rev Canon E. Roberts. Interestingly, Mrs Corrigan was wife of Major T.W.E. Corrigan, who was Honorary Secretary at Moelfre lifeboat station.

Meurig Davies served as Coxswain from 1971 to 1994. (By courtesy of the RNLI)

The handing over ceremony for the new D class inflatable D-250 on 12 July 1977. (By courtesy of the RNLI)

D-250 bringing in a broken down speed boat in the early 1980s. (By courtesy of Llandudno RNLI)

In August 1977 *Lilly Wainwright* and her crew completed a fine service. When the yacht *Dyllys* got into difficulties twelve miles north of Llandudno while on passage from Port St Mary to Holyhead, on the afternoon of 4 August, *Lilly Wainwright* was launched at 4.30pm. In extremely rough seas and a force eight south-westerly gale, with torrential rain, which greatly reduced visibility, the lifeboat crew battled their way out, reaching the casualty at 8.10pm. The Royal Fleet Auxiliary vessel *White Rover* was standing by *Dyllys* and provided a lee while the lifeboat was manoeuvred near the yacht. A line was thrown across by the lifeboat crew and secured and, slowly, the tow got under way, enabling *White Rover* to continue on her passage. The lifeboat and her tow arrived in Llandudno Bay at 11.10pm, but no suitable mooring was available so, as the weather was forecast to deteriorate,

Pictured with Lilly Wainwright in the early 1970s are, left to right, Christmas Tudno Jones (Second Coxswain), Tom Taylor (Honorary Secretary), Tony Frost and Bob Jones (Mechanic). Chris Jones and Bob Jones were great grandsons of Llandudno's first Coxswain, Hugh Jones. (By courtesy of Llandudno RNLI)

Lilly Wainwright bringing in a yacht on 28 September 1977 at the end of a three-hour service. The lifeboat launched at 11am after the sailing boat was seen drifting about ten miles north-west of the Great Orme. The lifeboat crew spotted the blue 18ft boat an hour and a half after launching, and found nobody was aboard as it appeared to have broken from its moorings.

Relief 37ft Oakley lifeboat Vincent Nesfield being launched on lifeboat day in August 1978. (By courtesy of Llandudno RNLI)

Lilly Wainwright on her carriage outside the lifeboat house. (By courtesy of Llandudno RNLI)

with the gale force winds veering to the north-west, it was decided to tow the yacht round the Great Orme to Deganwy, where the yacht was safely moored at 2am. The lifeboat returned to station at 3.15am having been at sea for nearly eleven hours. For this excellent service, a Letter of Appreciation, signed by Captain Nigel Dixon, RN, the Director of the RNLI, was later sent to Coxswain Meurig Davies and his crew.

Various changes took place at the station during 1977 and 1978. In December 1977 the Fowler Challenger III tractor T56 was replaced by a new and more powerful Case 1150B1 tractor,

Sequence of photos showing the recovery of Lilly Wainwright on the beach. (By courtesy of Joan Hughes)

T86; this served the station for the next ten years. In 1978 Thomas Taylor retired as Honorary Secretary, and was succeeded by Lt Cdr Edward Yates. To mark his thirty years of devoted service, Mr Taylor was presented with a Bar to his Gold Badge at the RNLI's Annual General Meeting in 1979.

During May 1981 the Llandudno lifeboat volunteers had a busy couple of days. On 23 May the inshore lifeboat D-250 was launched at 12.25pm to a dinghy, powered by an outboard engine, which had broken down a mile and a half off the Little Orme. The crew of two were rescued and their dinghy was towed ashore at 1.30pm. The ILB was launched again at 3.52pm, going this time to a sailing dinghy which had capsized a mile off Rhos-on-Sea. In choppy seas and a force six south-westerly wind, a local boat rescued the yachtsman who was then transferred to the ILB to be landed ashore. Later that evening, D-250 was called out again, being launched at 7.40pm after a dinghy had been reported overturned, but nothing was found and the ILB returned ashore at 9.10pm.

The following day D-250 was in action again, being launched first at 12.15pm to the yacht *Bon Ami*, which was being towed

by a motor boat, leaving the ILB to land a sick member of the yacht's crew. As the ILB returned to help moor the yacht in Llandudno Bay, the lifeboat crew received a radio message from the Coastguard asking for their help with a dinghy which had capsized off the Little Orme. The sole occupant was rescued and the dinghy righted and towed ashore, enabling the lifeboat crew to return and help moor *Bon Ami*; the ILB finally returned ashore at 1.45pm. She was called out again at 7.05pm that evening, to a small yacht which was in difficulties two miles off the Pier. The yacht, with two crew on board, was towed ashore at 7.30pm. The ILB was launched for a third time that day, at 10.45pm, after a report that red flares had been sighted off Old Colwyn. But nothing was found and so the ILB returned to station again at 12.15am.

Lilly Wainwright launching on exercise in 1980 with a crew numbering ten on board. (By courtesy of Llandudno RNLI)

Lifeboat crew in the lifeboat house, from left to right, Gordon Short (tractor driver), Ian McNeil, Meurig Davies (Coxswain), Glyn David Jones (Head Launcher), Hugh Hughes, Adrian Dunkley (Mechanic), David Noakes and Lionel Collis.

In the early hours of 30 December 1981 news was received that the 18ft cabin cruiser *Surf Power* had broken down 200 yards off Rhos Point in choppy seas and a force five north-easterly wind. The relief ILB D-205 was launched at 2.25am, but as the volunteer crew knew that they would be operating in total darkness very close inshore *Lilly Wainwright* was also launched, putting out at 2.40am to provide back up. D-205 reached the casualty at 2.45am and took her in tow, and then anchored it off the sailing club slipway and landed the crew of two. On seeing the sea conditions on the slipway, the owner of the cabin cruiser was taken back out to his boat, which was then towed ashore, with the ILB being beached at Rhos. The launching trolley was taken from Llandudno by road for the ILB, and *Lilly Wainwright* returned to station at 4am.

During 1982–83 work on extending the lifeboat house, built eighty years earlier, was undertaken. The extension, at the back of the house, was built to enable the Unimog towing vehicle, used with the ILB, to be accommodated. The rebuilt boathouse

Relief 37ft Oakley lifeboat J.G. Graves of Sheffield being recovered in October 1985, wih Lilly Wainwright just visible (to the left in upper photo). The Relief lifeboat, which was the first 37ft Oakley to be built, spent a week at Llandudno. (By courtesy of the RNLI)

was formally opened in June 1984 during a ceremony which was performed by George Scarth, of Pudsey, who had made a substantial donation towards the cost, in memory of his wife, Edith.

Later in the summer, on 4 August 1984, D-250 and her volunteer crew had a busy day. She was launched at 12.10pm after a party of canoeists were reported in difficulties 200 yards off the Orme's Head lighthouse. Of the three canoes, two had capsized several times and were full of water. By the time the ILB arrived the three canoeists were suffering from exposure and so they were pulled out of the water. The ILB then headed towards the West Shore to land them, requesting an ambulance to meet the ILB when she got ashore. But then another capsized canoe was seen, so the occupant of that was also rescued. As the ILB carried on towards the shore, a further nine canoeists were seen, so the ILB crew advised them to keep together, close inshore. The ILB then made for the shore to land the four people, while a helicopter watched the other canoes until they were safe. Once the four canoeists had been landed and taken to a waiting ambulance, D-250 put to sea again and the four abandoned canoes were recovered, after which the ILB was beached at Deganwy at 2pm and taken back to station by road.

In November 1984 *Lilly Wainwright* was taken for a routine overhaul at Dickie's Boatyard, Bangor, while *Vincent Nesfield* came to Llandudno, and stayed until 23 July 1985, launching four times on service and saving one life during her nine-month stint. *Vincent Nesfield* was launched at 11.17am on 21 April 1985 to assist the ILB,

The crew pictured with Lilly Wainwright next to the lifeboat house. They are, left to right: George Scarth (donor), Meurig Davies (Coxswain), Tony Frost (Second Coxswain), Dave Noakes (Second Mechanic), Bryn Jones, Hughie Hughes, Gordon Short (tractor driver), Ian McNeil, Bob Smith, Glyn Chambers and John Roberts.

D class inflatable D-359 41 Club 1 served at Llandudno from 1988 to 1996. (By courtesy of Llandudno RNLI)

which had been called out to the yacht *Juno*, with five people on board, which was disabled three miles west of the Great Orme. Two people were taken off the yacht by the relief lifeboat and a tow line was secured; the yacht was towed safely to Conwy and the lifeboat returned to Llandudno at 3.35pm. The relief lifeboat was called out again on 24 May 1985, being launched at 1.06pm, to the aid of a speedboat which had broken down two miles off Llandudno. The boat's sole occupant was rescued and his boat towed ashore by the lifeboat at 1.37pm.

Lilly Wainwright returned in July 1985 and over the next couple of years undertook a few routine services. But she had to be taken away again in May 1988, this time for major hull repairs to be carried out after significant defects had been found. In her place, the relief 37ft Oakley class lifeboat *Calouste Gulbenkian* was placed on temporary duty, arriving on 23 May 1988 and remaining until 18 December 1989. *Lilly Wainwright* was taken by road to FBM Marine at Cowes, on the Isle of White, where much of her hull was completely rebuilt with new planking.

Lily Wainwright being recovered on Llandudno's West Shore in the 1970s, with Case 1150B tractor T86. (By courtesy of Llandudno RNLI)

Above: Relief 37ft Oakley lifeboat Calouste Gulbenkian returning from a service to a yacht on 24 July 1988. Built in 1961, the Relief boat had served at Weston-super-Mare and was on duty at Llandudno from May 1988 until December 1989. (By courtesy of Roger Swanston)

Left: Calouste Gulbenkian on display on the Promenade, 14 September 1989. (Nicholas Leach)

Just four days after she arrived, the Relief lifeboat undertook her first service, launching at 11pm on 27 May, after the Coastguard had reported that a man was stranded on the cliffs on the Little Orme. The lifeboat crew used the searchlight to illuminate the cliffs and the man was hauled up to safety by the Cliff Rescue Team, the lifeboat returning to station at 1.45am. On the evening of 1 July 1988 the Coastguard reported that the fishing vessel *Sarah Jane* had broken down off the Orme's Head. *Calouste Gulbenkian* was launched at 8.48pm, and found the casualty thirteen miles north-west of Llandudno. A towline was secured and the disabled boat was towed to Conwy.

In 1988 a new D class inflatable ILB was sent to Llandudno. She was one of the new Avon/Evans EA16 type, which had been

An aerial view of the lifeboat house in Lloyd Street, which was built in 1904 and enlarged in 1982-83. The extension at the rear can be clearly seen in this photo. (By courtesy of the RNLI)

designed by the RNLI to replace the earlier types of inflatable ILB. At a ceremony on 17 July 1988, a new ILB, D-359, was formally handed over to the station. The boat had been provided out of funds raised by the 41 Club, and was named *41 Club I*. Councillor Russell Gradwell, chairman of the station branch, welcomed the guests, and past president of the 41 Club, Andy Wallace, formally handed over the new inflatable to the RNLI; the Institution was represented by Peter Williams, area organiser and instigator of the appeal. The service of dedication was conducted by the Rector of Llandudno, the Rev Derek Richards, after which the ILB was launched to demonstrate her abilities in the choppy seas.

In rough seas and a south-westerly gale, a dinghy, with two men on board, got into difficulties off Rhos Point on 12 August 1988 and *Calouste Gulbenkian* was launched at noon to help. She reached

The Unimog vehicle was used to launch the inshore lifeboat from 1984 until 1994; it is pictured on the promenade in September 1989. The lifeboat house was extended in 1983-84 in order to accommodate the vehicle. It was one of the units used during the North Wales floods of in February 1990. (Nicholas Leach)

The crew with Lilly Wainwright are, left to right: Gordon Short, Bob Jones (Mech), Bryn Jones, Dennis Heritage, Glyn Jones, Ken Lathom, John Dickens, Jim Western, John Roberts, Chris Jones (Second Cox), Ray Williams and Tony Frost. (By courtesy of Llandudno RNLI)

A postcard view of Lilly Wainwright on display on the promenade.

The Talus MB-H launching tractor T102 on display on the promenade in September 1989. Built in 1987, T102 was stationed at Llandudno until 1999. (Nicholas Leach)

Above: Lilly Wainwright on her carriage on the Promenade in 1987. The Case 1150B launching tractor T86 served the station from December 1977 to 1987. (By courtesy of Llandudno RNLI)

Right: Lilly Wainwright crossing Mostyn Street on way back to boathouse. (By courtesy of Llandudno RNLI)

the casualty at 12.52pm, eight miles north-east of Llandudno, and saved the two men, while their dinghy was taken in tow to Rhos. The relief lifeboat saved another person on 21 June 1989, launching at 8.52am to the aid of the yacht *Tranquillity*, which was disabled with steering gear failure, off the West Shore. She was aground on a sandbank and so the lifeboat waited for the tide to rise and then went alongside so that two of the lifeboat crew being put could go board to help. After a tow line was secured, the yacht was towed to Conwy, and the lifeboat returned to Llandudno at 1.45pm.

On 26 February 1990 the north coast of Wales suffered serious flooding, with the towns of Towyn, Pensarn and Kinmel Bay being particularly badly affected. Hundreds of people were stranded in their homes when the sea broke through the coastal defences and swept in, covering a very large area. The ILBs from Llandudno, Rhyl and Flint were called out to help with the evacuation of the stranded people. The conditions which greeted the lifeboat crews were extremely challenging, with floodwater up to 6ft deep in places and currents of up to five knots. There were masses of floating debris in the area and countless underwater obstructions, ranging from collapsed walls, to open manhole covers, while some street lights were 'live' beneath the water. Working closely with the other emergency services in the area, Llandudno's Unimog and Flint's Land Rover also provided considerable assistance. The crews of the three ILBs ended up helping to bring about 580 people to safety, many elderly, sick or disabled, between 26 February and 1 March. Some of the lifeboat crews spent up to nineteen hours a day working in the dreadful conditions. The Chairman of the RNLI later sent special Certificates of Thanks to all the crews and shore helpers, numbering no fewer than fifty-one volunteers, from the three lifeboat stations involved.

Lifeboat volunteers wade through the flooded streets of North Wales in February 1990, using the ILB to help stranded people to safety. (By courtesy of the RNLI)

Llandudno's inshore lifeboat D-359 41 Club 1, one of three ILBs to help with the flooding, making her way through the Towyn floods carrying lifeboat men and firemen, with an RAF rescue helicopter hovering overhead, February 1990. (By courtesy of the RNLI)

Above: Lilly Wainwright in her twilight years, after being fitted with radar mast having had her aft cockpit enclosed. (By courtesy of Llandudno RNLI)

Lilly Wainwright towards the end of her service career, pictured probably at a boatyard, possibly Tyrrells Yard at Arklow. (By cortesy of the RNLI)

Lilly Wainwright returned to Llandudno just before Christmas 1989, but she spent less than another year at the station before being replaced in November 1990. On 26 November 1990 she was taken across the Irish Sea to Tyrrells Yard at Arklow, and on 25 January 1991 was placed on temporary station duty at Kilmore Quay. After being withdrawn from Kilmore Quay in December 1992, she was taken to Crosshaven Boatyard, near Cork, and from there was sold out of RNLI service in October 1993 to Cobh Heritage Trust Ltd. She has since been taken into private ownership and been restored, retaining her original name and in good condition.

Andy Pearce

I n November 1990 a new 12m Mersey class lifeboat arrived at Llandudno. Named *Andy Pearce*, she was different from any of the station's previous lifeboats in every respect, being faster, better equipped, and giving far better protection for the volunteer crew, thus enabling safer operations. Llandudno's Mersey was the sixth of the class to be built, and one of ten built from aluminium; the other Merseys, of which there were twenty-seven, were constructed from fibre reinforced composite (FRC).

The Mersey was developed as a carriage-launched lifeboat that was faster than existing carriage-launched lifeboats, such as the 37ft Oakley. With fast afloat and slipway lifeboats in service around the UK and Ireland, the Mersey's introduction meant that a fast lifeboat type suitable for every station could be provided by the RNLI, and it enabled the Institution to fulfil its aim of having fast lifeboats in service at every station by the early 1990s.

12m Mersey Andy Pearce on trials prior to coming to Llandudno. (By courtesy of the RNLI)

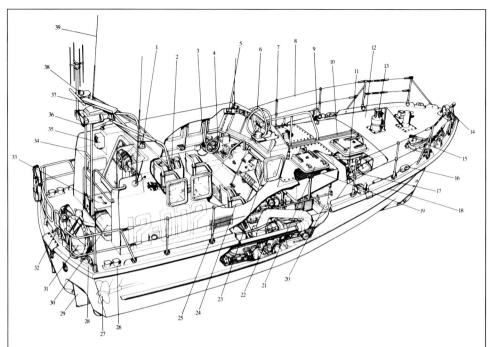

Cutaway drawing of 12m Mersey • Key: (1) Compass, (2) Torches, (3) Intercom, (4) Steering wheel, (5) Echo sounder, (6) DF loop, (7) Stanchion, (8) Guard wires, (9) Loudspeaker, (10) Boathook, (11) Fire extinguisher, (12) Non-slip deck paint, (13) Capstan, (14) Fairlead, (15) Anchor, (16) Starboard fairlead fitting, (17) Stretcher, (18) Fendering, (19) Fend-off, (20) Watertight door, (21) Watertight hatch, (22) Main engine, (23) Radar, (24) Seat, (25) Engine room air-filter, (26) Bollard, (27) Propeller, (28) Stern fairlead, (29) Rudder, (30) Liferaft, (31) Drogue, (32) Breeches buoy, (33) Access hatch, (34) Mast, (35) Capsize valve, (36) Navigation light, (37) Radar scanner, (38) Blue flashing light, (39) Whip aerial.

The first lifeboat type adopted by the RNLI that was faster than the displacement-hulled nine-knot craft built hitherto was the Waveney class. Based on a USCG design, it was introduced to the RNLI fleet in the mid-1960s and, over the next twenty years, almost all of the RNLI's afloat and slipway launched lifeboats were replaced by boats capable of speeds up to eighteen knots, with the Arun and Tyne lifeboats becoming mainstays of the fleet.

The Mersey design was developed during the 1980s as a fast carriage lifeboat (FCB). Because it had to be of a size suitable to fit in existing boathouses and be launched by the same method as the Oakleys and Rothers then in service, and which were to be replaced, its size and weight had to be kept within certain parameters. These design considerations led to a boat of 38ft in length, with a beam of 12ft 6in, powered by twin engines driving twin propellers that were protected in partial tunnels. The prototype, which never saw service and was only used for trials, was built of aluminium and the first two operational boats were also of aluminium, while the third operational boat was made

Andy Pearce in build at FBM, Cowes, February 1990, with the aluminium hull being prepared for fitting out. (Jeff Morris)

Mrs Pearce, donor of the lifeboat, talking to Coxswain Meurig Davies at the self-righting trial of the new lifeboat on 19 July 1990. (Jeff Morris)

The self-righting trial of Mersey lifeboat Official Number 1164, allocated to Llandudno,19 July 1990. The boat is hauled over by a crane, and the strops are released, leaving the boat free to right herself, which took about six seconds.

Llandudno crew on board Andy Pearce as she prepares to leave the RNLI Headquarters in Poole in November 1990. Five of the eight pictured formed the passage crew to North Wales. (By courtesy of the RNLI)

The passage crew on board Andy Pearce as she makes her way to North Wales, left to right: Lionel Collis, Meurig Davies, Robin Holden, Graham Heritage and Glyn Chambers. (By courtesy of Llandudno RNLI)

from fibre reinforced composite (FRC). While this latter boat was being subjected to significant, and successful, testing, a further eight aluminium hulls were completed including, in 1990, official number 1164 at the Cowes boatyard of FBM Ltd, which was allocated to Llandudno and named *Andy Pearce*.

Power came from two 285hp Caterpillar 3208T engines giving a speed of over seventeen knots. The design was self-righting by virtue of a watertight wheelhouse, which containing seating for a crew of six, plus an additional seat for an extra crew member or doctor. To enable the boat to be launched and recovered across a beach, the hull form incorporated tunnels and extended bilge keels to support the boat on the beach and protect the propellers and twin spade rudders. The design was designated the Mersey class.

In November 1988 the RNLI's Chief of Operations wrote to the Honorary Secretary that a Mersey class lifeboat had been allocated to the station, and so preparations began for its arrival. Alterations were required to the boathouse in Lloyd Street, occupied since 1903, and these were partly funded through the generosity of George Scarth of Pudsey, West Yorkshire, a longstanding supporter of the station, who also funded the GPS system on the new boat. The building had already been significantly extended a few years earlier, but further alterations were needed.

Andy Pearce was completed in October 1990 and sailed to the RNLI Depot in Poole at the end of the month for trials and crew training. Although a number of legacies contributed to her cost, the bulk came from the estate of Andrew Pearce on the express wish of his mother. Andrew, along with his brother Christopher, sadly died at a relatively young age. Their mother, Mrs Diana Pearce, having suffered a very tragic loss, followed the new boat's construction progress with great interest. Christopher Pearce's estate funded Holyhead's Severn class lifeboat, which was completed in 2003.

Self-righting trials took place at Cowes, where the boat had been built, on 19 July 1990, with Coxswain Meurig Davies and Honorary Secretary Ted Yates in attendance, along with donor Mrs Diana Pearce. Following final fitting out and testing, the boat then embarked on her forty-hour trials on 25 September 1990, with Staff Coxswain/Mechanic Mike McHugh in command, Trials Engineer Ian Campbell in charge of machinery, and, from Llandudno, Second Coxswain Ian (Dan) Jones, Mechanic Lionel Collis and Emergency Mechanic K. Jones on board. The new boat left Cowes and the trials began on 1 October, with calls at

Andy Pearce at Conwy after her passage from Poole in November 1990. On board are, left to right, Graham Heritage, Lionel Collis (Mechanic), Robin Holden and Meurig Davies (Coxswain). (By courtesy of Llandudno RNLI)

Brixham, Salcombe and Weymouth, and she reached the RNLI's Headquarters at Poole on 5 October 1990.

Crew training took place at Poole during early November 1990, with eight of Llandudno's crew learning about the capabilities of the new lifeboat, and the equipment. Coxswain Meurig Davies, Mechanic Lionel Collis, Second Mechanic Graham Heritage, Robin Holden, Glyn Chambers, Bob Smith, Brian Middlehurst and Les Jones came to Poole, with the latter three returning to station at the end of the week. On 6 November *Andy Pearce* set sail for her home station with Divisional Inspector George Rawlinson, who had only recently joined the RNLI, in command, and RNLI Divisional Engineer Brian Moss in charge of machinery. The passage took the boat via Weymouth, Fowey, Padstow, Fishguard, Dun Laoghaire, Holyhead and Conwy.

During the trip home, *Andy Pearce* and her passage crew were involved in a rescue as was leaving Padstow Fishguard. With heavy surf coming over the infamous Doom Bar at the entrance to the harbour, the lifeboat had to waited for a gap in the wave sets in order to get across, as did a number of fishing boats. As the lifeboat was waiting, her crew saw a small crabber being hit by a large breaking wave, which smashed the wheelhouse window, resulting in the skipper's face being severely injured. As the crabber cleared the surf line, she sheared to port, and her crew frantically summoned for help. Though the breaking surf was building all the time, Coxswain Meurig Davies and Deputy Divisional Inspector George Rawlinson took *Andy Pearce* through the surf and alongside the crabber, despite the rough conditions, long enough to transfer a first aider, Robin Holden, to the stricken vessel. He was able to stem the bleeding and stabilise the injured skipper, who was returned to Padstow and transferred to a waiting ambulance.

The rest of the passage was without major incident, and on 15 November 1990 *Andy Pearce* arrived at Llandudno, dressed

Andy Pearce, dressed overall, arives at Llandudno for the first time, 23 November 1990. (By courtesy of Llandudno RNLI)

Andy Pearce is recovered for the first time at Llandudno on 15 November 1990, with her predecessor Lilly Wainwright on her carriage nearby. (Tony Denton)

Andy Pearce is recovered at Llandudno after her arrival on station on 15 November 1990, with her predecessor Lilly Wainwright nearby on her carriage. (Tony Denton)

overall, to be greeted by many well-wishers and supporters of the station, who turned out in their hundreds despite rather inclement weather. The new lifeboat was recovered on the slipway at Llandudno's North Shore, and there followed a period of intensive training. With this successfully completed, the new lifeboat was formally declared operational on 23 November 1990.

Andy Pearce's first service came on 16 April 1991 when she went to the converted ship's lifeboat *Dizzy Lizzy* which had suffered machinery failure off Rhos on Sea in force seven north-easterly winds. Under the command of Cox Meurig Davies, the lifeboat took two men off the casualty, with the lifeboat suffering minor damage. In view of the severity of the conditions, the casualties were taken to Deganwy, which was more sheltered, and the lifeboat was recovered from the West Shore, having launched from the North Shore. This was the first time in living memory of the serving crew that this had occurred.

Andy Pearce (on right) with her predecessor Lilly Wainwright on the Promenade. On the new lifeboat are Dave Roberts and Graham Heritage; standing, left to right, are: Dan McCarthy, Brian Middlehurst, Pat Weir, Paul Conway, Les Jones, Ian MacNeil, Gareth Roberts, Tony Frost, Lionel Collis, Dan Jones, Meurig Davies, Les Lloyd-Jones, Gordon Short, Robin Holden, Nigel Forrest. (By coutesy of Llandudno RNLI)

Andy Pearce is hauled into the lifeboat house on Lloyd Street for the first time, 23 November 1990, to be carefully rehoused. The building had been designed for a 37ft sailing lifeboat, not a 12m aluminium-hulled craft and launching tractor, and housing the Mersey left little extra space inside. (Jeff Morris)

During May 1991 Llandudno's Second Coxswain Dan Jones was one of the crew who sailed the relief Mersey class lifeboat *Marine Engineer* from Poole to Oslo for the International Lifeboat Conference, a gathering of lifeboat services from around the world to share and exchange information and technical expertise. It was a senior crew aboard the boat, manned by Staff Coxswain Michael Houchens and District Engineer A. Watling, along with Wells-next-the-Sea Coxswain/Mechanic Graham Walker, and Ilfracombe Mechanic Andrew Putt.

On 18 June 1991 *Andy Pearce* was formally named by HRH the Duchess of Kent. The rain showers did not dampen the spirits of those present, with the rain easing for the ceremony as hundreds of spectators braved the elements. The occasion was chaired by Councillor Russell Gradwell, the station's long-standing Chairman, together with Lt Cdr Ted Yates, Honorary Secretary. The Duchess received a special souvenir programme from coxswain's son, Gareth Davies, and a posy from Jodie Frost, daughter of the head launcher, before taking her place in a shelter on the podium.

The lifeboat was largely funded from the estate of the late Andy Pearce and, in a short speech, his mother, Mrs Diana Pearce, said: 'Andy was always there when he was needed, and we are proud to think this lifeboat that bears his name will also be on hand whenever someone needs help at sea.' In accepting the new boat, Ted Yates recalled the station's proud lifeboat tradition and paid tribute to all who had served in the crew. The Duchess of Kent expressed her pleasure at being asked, once again, to carry out the naming of a lifeboat and she pressed the button to release the champagne, which broke over *Andy Pearce's* bow. Donning a yellow jacket, the Duchess joined the crew under the command of Coxswain Meurig Davies for a demonstration of the lifeboat's capabilities, taking the helm herself for part of the trip.

Andy Pearce served at Llandudno for over a quarter of a century, launching more than 350 times on service and carrying out rescues

Before the naming ceremony of Andy Pearce on 18 June 1991, Duchess of Kent meets Lionel Collis, Graham Heritage, Robin Holden, Glyn Chambers, Gordon Short, Tony Frost and Hughie Hughes. (By courtesy of Llandudno RNLI)

The platform party for the naming ceremony of Andy Pearce, 18 June 1991. (Jeff Morris)

At the end of her naming ceremony, Andy Pearce is launched, with HRH Duchess of Kent on board, for a short demonstration run. (Jeff Morris)

Andy Pearce being lanched at the end of her naming ceremony, 18 June1991, with invited guests on board. (Jeff Morris)

to a wide variety of craft, large and small. She did occasionally assist and support commercial coasting vessels, such as on 18 June 1992, exactly a year after her naming, when she launched to assist the coaster *Residu*, which was taking on water twenty-five miles north of Llandudno. When the ship's list increased, it was decided to take the crew off by helicopter. *Andy Pearce* and her crew stood by once the crew had been lifted off and retrieved the ship's automatic alarm to prevent another rescue effort being triggered by it going off. The ship sank a few hours later.

On 12 March 1993 *Andy Pearce* was asked to stand by the Kilkeel-based fishing vessel *Solitaire*, which had a large German magnetic mine caught in its net. *Andy Pearce* was launched under the command of Coxswain Meurig Davies at 2.25pm, reaching the

casualty at 3pm. The fishing vessel was then escorted closer inshore and anchored, and the five crew taken off while bomb disposal experts undertook an inspection and then lowered it to the sea bed, with *Andy Pearce* being recovered at 11pm after many hours at sea. The following day, at the request of the Bomb Disposal Team and the Coastguard, *Andy Pearce* towed the mine, which was buoyed on airbags, out to sea beyond the Constable Bank, a few miles north of the Great Orme's Head. The mine was then lowered to the seabed and the lifeboat stood by, two miles away, while it was detonated.

On 3 June 1993 Llandudno suffered unprecedented flooding caused by concentrated heavy rainfall in the area. The lifeboat house was flooded with 4ft of water after hours of torrential rain, which also flooded the whole town. The all-weather lifeboat was already on display on the promenade, and the ILB was used to help evacuate numerous people who were stranded in homes which had been flooded. The boathouse was used by the Coastguard, whose own building was unusable, as a temporary operational base.

On 11 February 1995, with Coxswain Dan Jones in command, *Andy Pearce* was launched at 3.15pm in poor visibility and south-westerly force six winds to assist the 30ft yacht *Blaze*, which had engine failure. Finding the yacht north of Rhyl, the lifeboat established a tow and the vessel was taken towards Llandudno Bay. However, the Coxswain was unhappy leaving the craft there, so it was towed to Conwy Marina, where berthing problematic in the strong winds. The casualty was therefore taken to Conwy Quay, which was more sheltered, and the lifeboat returned to station, her crew having been with her at sea for about six hours.

Presentation to Mrs Diana Pearce following the naming ceremony of Andy Pearce. Standing, left to right, are: Dan McCarthy, Dave Roberts, Hughie Hughes, Dan Jones, Pat Weir, Graham Heritage, Alan Bayliff, Lionel Collis, Les Lloyd-Jones, Meurig Davies, Glyn Chambers, Bryn Jones, Mrs Pearce, Brian Middlehurst, Ian MacNeil, Nigel Forrest, John Crawford, Martin Crawford, Paul Conway. Seated, left to right, are: Bob Smith, Gordon Short, Robin Holden, Kevin Jones, Carl Davies. (By courtesy of Llandudno RNLI)

Crew members Nigel Forrest, Dave Jones, Robbie Shields, Robin Holden and Glyn Chambers with members of the Ladies Guild in the mid-1990s. (By courtesy of Llandudno RNLI)

Llandudno lifeboat crew, early 1990s; on board Andy Pearce, left to right, are: Robin Holden, Graham Heritage, Lionel Collis (Mechanic), Dan Jones (Second Coxswain) and Meurig Davies (Coxswain); standing, left to right: Gordon Short, Glyn Chambers, Les Jones, Dan McCarthy, Bob Smith, Nick Frost, Tony Frost, Hughie Hughes, Dave Roberts, Alan Bayliff, Les Lloyd-Jones. Les Lloyd-Jones was the last of generations of Lloyd-Jones to be involved with Llandudno lifeboat. (Llandudno RNLI)

Below: Andy Pearce and D class inflatable D-346 during a first aid medical exercise. (By courtesy of the RNLI)

Later that year, on 1 July 1995, the 27ft yacht *Denise* called for help at 1.10am while moored alongside Llandudno's jetty on a falling tide with a surf running and a force five north-easterly wind blowing into the bay. Coxswain Ian Jones showed great skill in manoeuvring *Andy Pearce* astern in shallow water to pull the casualty and her crew away from danger and prevent her from breaking up. The yacht was taken to Conwy marina, after which the lifeboat returned to station, with the volunteer shore crew facing an arduous low-water recovery.

On 20 October 1996 a new inshore lifeboat, D-508, was named *John Saunderson* by Dr Barbara Saunderson, the first of three ILBs to be provided through her generosity. The station's ILBs have always been relatively busy. The bulk of their services involve small pleasure boats, swimmers, kayakers, rock fishermen and small yachts. On many occasions, the ILBs and their crews are requested to assist emergency services deal distressed people or, sadly, body recoveries. In the summer months, the station's ILBS are regularly

Andy Pearce departing for Conwy River Festival. On board are, left to right, Goronwy Owen, Glyn Jones and Dennis Heritage; standing, left to right: Meurig Davies, Gareth Roberts, Les Jones, Glyn Chambers, Alan Bayliff, Keith Charlton, Lionel Collis, Gordon Short, Graham Heritage, Hughie Hughes, Dan Jones, Mark Westwood, Nicki Frost, Pat Weir and Brian Middlehurst. (By courtesy of Llandudno RNLI)

Meurig Davies retired as Coxswain in 1994 at the age of fifty-five after thirty years of service, and was succeeded by Dan Jones. (By courtesy of the RNLI)

called to people cut off by the tide, mostly on the West Shore, where a deep channel running close inshore between the Great Orme and Deganwy, known as the North Deep, floods two hours after low water, and walkers can easily get stranded. People who get caught out, usually holidaymakers unaware of the dangers, then try to cross the channel, endangering themselves. The fatality of a teenager in 1996 had a lasting effect on the crew and there has always been a keenness to respond quickly to West Shore calls.

On 24 August 1997 an 18ft boat was reported overdue at 11pm. The conditions were excellent as the SAR operation commenced,

The naming ceremony of John Saunderson (D-508) on 20 October 1996 with Lt Cdr John MacDonald (Honorary Secretary) to the right of the aerial, Lord Mostyn in the dark coat. Dr Saunderson is flanked by Les Jones to her right and Glyn Chambers and Jobi Hold to the left. On the far right is Chairman Russell Gradwell. (Llandudno RNLI)

The naming ceremony of the new inshore lifeboat John Saunderson (D-508), with Dr Barbara Saunderson pouring the champagne over the new ILB. (By courtesy of the RNLI)

Below: D class inflatable John Saunderson (D-508) being launched for the station's annual lifeboat day, August 2000. (Nicholas Leach)

involving both Llandudno and Rhyl lifeboats, joined at daylight by their respective ILBs and Beaumaris' Atlantic ILB. The weather was calm but the casualty, with two persons and their dog aboard, had been capsized by a rogue wave and sunk. One casualty was recovered by Rhyl lifeboat, but sadly neither his companion nor the dog were found. The lifeboat was at sea for over twenty-two hours under the command of Coxswain Dan Jones, with a brief break at Conwy Marina to refuel and relieve one crew member.

The hazards of carriage launching and recovery were evident on 13 October 1997 during an exercise launch at the North Shore slipway in a slight to moderate sea. Difficulty withdrawing the starboard forward pin delayed the 'knock out' of the chain. Crew

Andy Pearce being recovered at the North Shore. (By courtesy of Llandudno RNLI)

Crew dinner in the 1990s. Back row, left to right: Gareth Roberts, Dave Roberts, Kevin Jones, Pat Weir, John Haydon, Dan McCarthy, Carl Davies, Ian MacNeil. Middle row: Les Lloyd-Jones, Goronowy Owen, Hughie Hughes, Nicki Frost, Alan Bayliff, Nigel Forrest, Bob Smith, Martin Crawford, Dr J.J. Green. Seated, left to right: Graham Heritage, Dan Jones, Dr Norman Roberts, Meurig Davies, Ted Yates, Tony Frost, Lionel Collis. At front, left to right: Glyn Chambers, Robin Holden, Les Jones, and Brian Middlehurst. (By courtesy of Llandudno RNLI)

Relief 12 Mersey Fisherman's Friend being brought through the streets on 10 June 1996 and launched to go to Conwy Marina, where the crew were to take back station boat Andy Pearce after refit, and pass the relief lifeboat to the Rhyl crew. (Nicholas Leach)

Right: Relief 12 Mersey Fisherman's Friend at Conwy Marina alongside station boat Andy Pearce, having completed her refit. (Nicholas Leach)

Below: Rhyl lifeboat Lil Cunningham pictured from Fisherman's Friend as both boats head to Conwy, 10 June 1996. (Nicholas Leach)

member David 'Diddy' Jones, on the aft chain, seeing an issue, delayed his own 'knock out', which consequently put pressure on his chain. Seeing the issue being resolved, he attempted to knock out the retaining chain clip, but the hammer rebounded into his face, causing serious injuries. The boat, now in the water, was quickly recovered. David was taken to hospital for surgery and was unable to return to work for some months. To his credit, he subsequently returned to active service and remained a member of the crew. As a result of this accident, the RNLI conducted a thorough review of launching procedures for Mersey class lifeboats and introduced new national procedures.

On 27 January 2001, little more than three years after the accident involving David Jones, a completely different incident occurred when the boat was being taken down the slipway for a low water launch. The tractor was pulling the boat on its carriage when, with algae on the slipway, the tractor slipped and jack knifed, resulting in Second Coxswain Robin Holden, who was standing on the rear platform of the tractor, trapping his arm between the tractor and the boat. This too resulted in absence from employment and active service, but Robin duly returned to both after he had recovered from his injuries. This incident led to a decision for the boat to be pushed bow first by the tractor down the slipway and, again, a national change in procedure.

On 6 May 2004 *Andy Pearce* attended the naming ceremony of the new 17m Severn class lifeboat *Christopher Pearce* at Holyhead, as the new lifeboat had been funded by the same donors who had paid for Llandudno's boat, making it an historic occasion. *Christopher Pearce* had originally been due to call at Llandudno on 21 December 2003, a few days after the boat had arrived on station at Holyhead, but this was cancelled after *Andy Pearce* had been out on service during the night on what turned out to be a hoax call.

On 24 July 2004 the relief lifeboat *Mary Margaret* was on station and launched under the command of Dan Jones following

Andy Pearce being launched for the station's annual lifeboat day in August 2000 by Talus tractor T94, which was on station from 1999 to 2008. (Nicholas Leach)

Andy Pearce at speed off the beach during a demonstation run on the station's annual lifeboat day in August 2000. (Nicholas Leach)

Andy Pearce at speed during the station's annual lifeboat day, August 2000. (Nicholas Leach)

reports that the catamaran *Esmerelda* was taking in water twelve miles north of the Great Orme. The wind was south-westerly force five, it was raining and the seas were moderate. The lifeboat reached the scene just after 8pm, and Deputy Second Coxswain Graham Heritage and crew member Dave Davis were successfully transferred to the casualty, despite challenging conditions. Initially, they helped with bailing out the catamaran, and then the lifeboat's pump was transferred to control the flooding. In the meantime, a tow was established to take the catamaran towards Llandudno Bay. However, during the tow, the ingress of water was too great for the pump and the catamaran began to sink. Those on board were quickly recovered, the tow was abandoned and the catamaran was beached on the West Shore. The lifeboat was rehoused and ready for service at 3am after a long and challenging service. Subsequently, Michael Vlasto, RNLI Operations Director, wrote a letter of congratulation to Dan Jones, Graham Heritage and Dave Davis, thanking them for their efforts during this nine-hour service.

A life was saved by the ILB when a man was pulled from freezing seas during the evening of 3 October 2004 in almost gale force conditions. The man, in his 50s, was found 200 yards from the end of the town's pier; he had been fishing on the pier and had fallen into the sea. A crew member got into the water to help get the man into the ILB, which was coping with difficult conditions in fading light. The casualty was slipping in an out of consciousness and was taken to hospital immediately on being landed ashore.

On 17 October 2004 relief lifeboat *Mary Margaret* had to operate in shallow water when the skipper of the yacht *Mjolner,* with two men on board, misjudged the channel entrance to Conwy got into difficulty while the yacht was on passage from Liverpool. She was being pounded in shallow water near rocks off Penmaenmawr in rough conditions. Using local knowledge and the boat's Global Positioning System (GPS), the lifeboat crew approached the casualty through slightly deeper water in a gully and secured a line to haul the boat to safety before it was broken up, saving the two people on board. The owner of the boat, Ken Johnson, a violinist with the Liverpool Philharmonic Orchestra, was due to play at Llandudno's Venue Cymru that evening. Although somewhat shaken by his ordeal, he nevertheless fulfilled his agreed obligations with his waistcoat and tails still dry.

ILB crew members were involved in a rescue mission with a difference on 3 February 2005, when they helped an injured and distressed whale. The 6m creature was spotted off Penrhyn Bay having become entangled in a mooring rope. Two lifeboat crew and an RSPCA inspector aboard the ILB managed to reach the whale and cut it free, after which it headed to the open sea.

On 6 May 2004 Andy Pearce was taken to Holyhead to attend the naming ceremony of Christopher Pearce, that station's new 17m Severn, which was funded through the bequest of Christopher Pearce whose brother's estate had funded Andy Pearce. (Nicholas Leach)

In November 2006 the new D class inflatable D-656 William Robert Saunderson was placed on station. The new ILB was, like her predecessor, funded by Dr Barbara Saunderson, and was named during a ceremony on the promenade, as pictured, on 7 July 2007. (By courtesy of the RNLI)

Lifeboat crew on D class inflatable D-656 William Robert Saunderson with Father Christmas during a Christmas publicity and fund-raising event. (By courtesy of Llandudno RNLI)

On 27 August 2008 the lifeboat crew were involved in a long and arduous service under the command of Deputy Second Coxswain Graham Heritage. The yacht *Odyssey*, based in Conwy and on passage back to her home port from the Isle of Man, had been fouled by ropes and small buoys attached to fishing gear thirty miles north of the Great Orme in gale conditions and a heavy sea. Both of the yacht's crew were feeling the effects of the conditions in a dangerous situation. *Andy Pearce* was launched at 3pm having been on a ten-hour service the previous day. After just over two hours the lifeboat reached the yacht and crew member Tim James, wearing a drysuit, entered the water, and cut away the tangled ropes around the yacht's propeller and rudder. Tim then boarded the yacht and helped the skipper sail the boat to Puffin Island, where both yacht and lifeboat waited for the flood tide to enable the Conwy estuary to be entered. The yacht broached four times on the way, and the lifeboat was at sea for a total of sixteen hours. The RNLI's Director of Operations subsequently sent a Letter of Thanks to Tim James in recognition of his actions.

Photographs taken for an article in the RNLI's Lifeboat magazine on station succession planning in 2010. Pictured are, left to right, Glyn Chambers, Nigel Forrest, Assistant Coxswain Danny James, Coxswain Robin Holden, Second Coxswain Graham Heritage, Assistant Coxswain Tim James and Martin Thomas, in their lifeboat gear and for their day jobs. These are paint store manager, train driver, windfarm boat skipper, health service manager, heating and plumbing engineer, managing director and marina operative respectively. (Nigel Millard)

A few weeks later, on 8 September 2008, *Andy Pearce* was involved in a joint operation with Holyhead lifeboat *Christopher Pearce* to assist the Ocean Youth Trust's sail training vessel *Greater Manchester Challenge*, which had a seized engine ten miles off Llandudno. The lifeboat launched at 9pm into extremely choppy conditions. Once on scene, *Andy Pearce* and her crew transferred the tow to *Christopher Pearce* off Point Lynas so that the boat could be towed to Holyhead, its port of destination.

Dan Jones retired as Coxswain in 2009 and was succeeded by Second Coxswain Robin Holden, who held the post for two years before handing over to Second Coxswain Graham Heritage. On Graham's appointment, no Second Coxswain was appointed, so Robin Holden, David Davis, Tim James and Danny Jones acted as joint Assistant Coxswains.

In January 2011 the station was awarded a vellum to commemorate its 150th anniversary. The occasion was marked by a service of thanksgiving held at St John's Methodist Church. *Andy Pearce* was taken to the Church the previous evening and, on her

Llandudno lifeboat on service to Sea Griffin on 9 July 2007. It was a busy day for Andy Pearce, which was first called to the yacht which had a fouled anchor. Having put two crew members on board to assist, Andy Pearce was diverted to the yacht Sweet Jane which was aground, and stood by while Conwy ILB (pictured) towed the yacht clear. Andy Pearce returned to Sea Griffin and escorted both yachts to Conwy Marina. (By courtesy of Llandudno RNLI)

carriage, parked outside, making a somewhat unusual sight. In the same year, Dan Jones, then Head Launcher, was awarded the MBE.

During 2011 an RNLI shop was opened in Lloyd Street near the promenade and close to the town's main shopping area. As the lifeboat house was not open to the public, nor in a prominent place close to any retail outlets, the shop did much to raise the profile of the station as well as bring in funds for the RNLI. It has been manned by a dedicated group of volunteers since being opened, initially under the management of Lyn Brown, later being jointly run by Hazel Jowett, Eileen Bennett and Gill Baggs.

On the operational side, on 3 April 2012 the coaster *Carrier*, with a crew of seven, was loading limestone from Llanddulas Quarry as the weather worsened. As the coaster tried to leave the jetty, around 8pm she was swung broadside by the prevailing seas before she did not have sufficient power going astern to clear the jetty. As a result, she was swept aground onto the rock armour on the shoreline and

Talus MB-H tractor T91 was the last such launch tratcor to serve Llandudno. Built in 1982, it was the first of the RNLI's Talus MB-H vehicle, and served from 2008 to 2017. (Nicholas Leach)

Llandudno lifeboat crew, 2010; on tractor are Alan Bayliff and Glyn Chambers; on ALB are, left to right, Dave Davis, Jobi Hold, Robin Holden, Graham Heritage, Les Jones, Nigel Forrest, Danny Jones, Dave Roberts, Aled Williams, Dave Jones, Martin Jones, Sue Davies, Ian Appleton, Tim James. By the Land Rover are Steve Howard, Dan Jones, Keith Charlton; standing by the ILB are Andy Jones, Wes Jones, Kelsey Byrne, Luke Heritage and Mike Heritage. (Llandudno RNLI)

seas started to pound her heavily. The incident made the national news headlines because of concerns about fuel from ruptured tanks being sprayed over the nearby A55 dual carriageway, part of which had to be closed, causing traffic chaos in the area. Being close inshore, she also became something of an attraction for sightseers.

Under Coxswain Graham Heritage, *Andy Pearce* was launched, getting away only when there was a lull in the heavy surf crashing onto the North Shore from the northerly gale. Rhyl lifeboat *Lil Cunningham* arrived on scene just before *Andy Pearce*, but neither boat could provide any assistance and the coaster's crew were taken off by helicopter. The coaster could not be got off the rocks, and subsequently became a constructive total loss, being dismantled over several weeks at the site. For the first time in many years, *Andy Pearce* was recovered on the West Shore after this service due to the severity of the conditions on the North Shore.

On 1 June 2014 Llandudno lifeboat and her crew joined with Moelfre lifeboat *Kiwi* and her crew for a joint navigational exercise, which involved meeting at the position where HM Submarine

Moelfre lifeboat Kiwi (on left) and Llandudno Lifeboat Andy Pearce lay wreaths in Liverpool Bay on 1 June 2014 at the position where ninety-nine men lost their lives aboard HM Submarine Thetis seventy-five years earlier. (Jodi Kite)

Thetis had been lost in Liverpool Bay seventy-five years earlier, with the loss of the ninety-nine men aboard. At 1.40pm, the time that the boat had dived, both lifeboats laid wreaths on the spot before continuing with their exercise. At the same time, a memorial service was held at Birkenhead and a plaque unveiled to commemorate those who were lost and the four who were saved.

On 12 April 2015 both Llandudno lifeboats were launched to assist the 35ft yacht *Jeanneau,* which got into difficulty in Conwy Bay. The yacht, which was on passage from Conwy to Pwllheli with two persons on board, had left Conwy Marina early in the morning, but got into difficulty in the gale-force south-westerly winds which had created very rough seas on an ebbing tide. The yacht sent out a distress call although its plight had already been seen by local lifeboat personnel and reported to the Coastguard. The yacht, which had become extremely difficult for those on

Relief 12m Mersey Lady of Hilbre at Conwy Marina in October 2016 awaiting passage to Llandudno prior to taking up duty. Lady of Hilbre was a sister vessel to Andy Pearce, having been built at the same time; she served at Hoylake from 1990 to 2014. (By courtesy of Llandudno RNLI)

Andy Pearce beng lifted out of the water (below) to be placed on a low loader at Conwy Marina on 5 October 2016 (left) to go to Falmouth Boat Co for refit. (By courtesy of Llandudno RNLI)

Andy Pearce being brought out of the boathouse on Lloyd Street on exercise, June 2015. (Nicholas Leach)

Andy Pearce and D class inflatable D-656 being taken along Lloyd Street to the Promenade, June 2015. (Nicholas Leach)

Andy Pearce being launched on exercise, June 2015. (Nicholas Leach)

Andy Pearce being launched on a routine exercise, June 2015. (Nicholas Leach)

Andy Pearce heading out of the bay on a fine summer evening, June 2015. (Nicholas Leach)

Andy Pearce being recovered, with the skids being laid so she can be hauled out of the water, June 2015. (Nicholas Leach)

board to control, was driven east of the Great Orme's Head into Liverpool Bay in very confused seas. The ILB had been launched on exercise earlier but, due to the conditions, was operating within the confines of Llandudno Bay, out of the force of the gale.

The ILB was quickly relaunched as concerns were expressed that the yacht's crew might have been washed overboard while the vessel was broaching in the rough conditions a mile to the east of

An aerial view of the lifeboat house built in 1903 in Lloyd Street, surrounded by private houses and other buildings, some distance from the sea front. (By courtesy of the RNLI)

The lifeboat house built in 1903 in Lloyd Street, pictured in 2015 in its final operational guise, having been considerably altered since first being built. (Nicholas Leach)

the Great Orme. The ILB was subsequently recalled once those on board were confirmed safe and in view of the severity of the conditions. However, by this time, shortly after 10am, *Andy Pearce* had launched and was taken alongside the casualty long enough for Assistant Mechanic Aled Williams to jump across to help. The yacht was taken in tow to the lee of the Great Orme's Head and anchored. At this point it was decided that one of the yacht's two crew needed to be evacuated. The crew member was transferred to the lifeboat and, in the shelter of Llandudno Bay, transferred to the ILB to be brought ashore. Coxswain Graham Heritage, in consultation with the Coastguard, decided that the lifeboat should remain with the casualty in the lee of Great Orme's Head until tidal conditions allowed the yacht to be towed to Conwy Marine, with two lifeboat crew members on board. By this time the wind had eased, and the lifeboat was eventually recovered at 5pm, having spent almost seven hours at sea.

Llandudno lifeboat crew and station management team on the 25th anniversary of Andy Pearce's arrival at the station, November 2015. Standing, left to right: Ralph Hughes, Kelsey Byrne, Keith Charlton, Glyn Chambers, Dave Jones, Adam Finch-Saunders, Andy Jones, Ian Appleton, Robbie Shields, Dave Davies, Bert Williams, Steve Howard, Mike Jones, Vinny Hill, Aled Williams, Luke Heritage, Phill Howell, Simon Hajahmed, Dave Roberts, Nigel Forrest and Les Howell. Seated, left to right: Dr J.J. Green (Station Chairman), Arthur Barlow (Treasurer), Les Jones (Station Mechanic), Captain Marcus Elliott (LOM), Dan Jones (Head Launcher), Paul Moreton, Mike Knowles and Alun Pari Huws (Deputy Launching Authorities). (Alan Cudbertson).

On 15 November 2015, twenty-five years to the day since *Andy Pearce* arrived at the station, a reception was held at the Lloyd Street boathouse to mark the occasion, with the boat outside dressed overall. Although there was a stiff breeze, the rain held off and the temperature was above average for the time of year, for what was a memorable occasion for all station personnel who were present, together with Guild members, shop volunteers and invited guests.

D class inflatable Dr Barbara Saunderson (D-793) was placed on station on 6 June 2016. She was the seventh ILB to serve Llandudno since 1965. (Nicholas Leach)

Andy Pearce exercising with HMCG Rescue Helicopter 936 during Emergency Services Day on 13 August 2017. (By courtesy of Llandudno RNLI)

During 2016 *Andy Pearce* had one of her busiest years, launching on service twelve times and being on stand-by for a further three occasions. She went to the experimental 24m windfarm transfer vessel *Tenacity*, with ten persons on board, which had engine failure half a mile north of the Great Orme's Head and towed the vessel to Conwy Marina. The last service call of the year came on 3 October, the day before *Andy Pearce* was due to go by road to Falmouth for refit. She launched to a Kirkcudbright-based 80ft beam trawler, twenty-two miles north of the Great Orme's Head. The vessel had suffered engine failure and was drifting towards the Gwynt-y-Mor Windfarm. Another fishing vessel, also from Kirkcudbright, arrived on scene and was able to effect a slow tow northwards.

Andy Pearce's remaining time at Llandudno was relatively quiet, although during her last eighteen months on station she was captured on video film for posterity to commemorate the withdrawal of the station from Lloyd Street, marking the end of lifeboat operations from the centre of the town.

Andy Pearce joins Rhyl lifeboat Lil Cunningham (12-24) and Hoylake lifeboat (not pictured) on 9 April 2017 for a memorial ceremony, held at sea just off the lifeboat house at Rhyl, to honour the memory of former Rhyl Second Coxswain Gerald Hughes, who died in March 2017. (Nicholas Leach)

A new boathouse and a new lifeboat

O n 21 October 2017 Llandudno lifeboat station enjoyed not only another busy year but also celebrated the culmination of almost two decades of planning, when a new lifeboat house was officially opened and new 13m Shannon all-weather and D class inflatable inshore lifeboats were both named and dedicated in a unique triple celebration. The new lifeboat house, built at Craig-y-Don, at the eastern end of the promenade, provided state-of-the art facilities for the volunteer crew, something that had been needed ever since 12m Mersey *Andy Pearce* had arrived at the station. With the opening of the new building, and the entry into service of the new lifeboat, the station's facilities were brought into the twenty-first century.

Numerous proposals and plans for a new lifeboat station had been made during the previous two decades and more. The boathouse in Lloyd Street, completed in 1903, was a significant improvement on the previous one near the Railway Station, but by the latter part of the twentieth century was unsuitable for the

13m Shannon William F. Yates on her proving trial off the Dorset coast in December 2016 after her completion at the RNLI's All-Weather Lifeboat Centre, Poole. (By courtesy of the RNLI)

long-term future of the station, lacking modern crew facilities and sufficient space for lifeboats and launch vehicles.

In 1998 planning permission was formally submitted for a new lifeboat house on the promenade adjacent to the pier, with the intention of utilising an existing slipway. The proposed building, designed to complement the resort's Victorian features, included a shop and viewing gallery. Despite broad support, there were significant objections by influential parties concerned that the

The new lifeboat house at Craig-y-Don was built over the course of eighteen months starting in April 2016. With the contractors at the start of the build are, left to right, Bert Williams, Assistant Mechanic Luke Heritage, Mechanic Les Jones, Coxswain Graham Heritage, Mike Jones, Chris Martin, Lifeboat Operations Manager Marcus Elliott, Divisional Operations Manager Lee Firman, and Richard Wynne and Chris Wynne of Wynne Construction. (By courtesy of Llanduno RNLI)

development would impinge on the historical character of the promenade, and the proposal was rejected.

The RNLI continued to try to find a solution, with several alternative sites being considered. In May 2004 plans were unveiled for a house on reclaimed land on the beach beside the pier road and Promenade, but five months later this plan was also rejected because of the difficulty in getting permission to build next to the pier wall, which had Grade II listed building status. So protracted was the matter by this stage that there was a real fear that Llandudno could lose its offshore lifeboat. However, the RNLI's Coast Review of 2011 confirmed that Llandudno would remain an all-weather station, and efforts continued to find a new site that would be suitable.

Further sites were investigated, with one at Craig-y-Don, at the eastern end of the bay, close to the Little Orme, where Victorian features were not as prominent as the site near the pier. The new Shannon class and its powerful launch rig were capable enough to operate from this more exposed site, making it a workable proposition. Nevertheless, it was not until 2014 that planning permission was finally obtained for the scheme. While the new site was exposed in northerly and north-westerly gales, the capability of the new all-weather boat and equipment was sufficient to cope with this, while the ILB, which would be co-located in the building, was able to operate from a variety of launch sites, being taken by road as had been the case since it first came to the station.

Coxswain Graham Heritage, Mechanic Les Jones and Lifeboat Operations Manager Marcus Elliott at the site of the new boathouse in April 2015, just before construction work began. (By courtesy of Llanduno RNLI)

The new lifeboat house at Craig-y-Don provides a suitable home to the new Shannon class lifeboat William F. Yates and D class inshore lifeboat Dr Barbara Saunderson (D-793).

Launch and recovery trials at Craig-y-Don using the prototype FCB2 ON.1285, known as 'Effseabee Two', and the prototype Supacat Launch and Recovery System (SLRS) rig, July 2011. The trials took place at various states of the tide adjacent to the paddling pool at the eastern end of the Promenade. Their success proved that the site was a suitable one and the new lifeboat house was subsequently built there. (Tony Denton)

The prototype FCB2, known as 'Effseabee Two', being launched during trials at Craig-y-Don, July 2011. (Tony Denton)

In July 2011 the Shannon prototype, designated 'FCB2', came to the site in order for launch and recovery trials to be conducted on the shingle beach close to where the proposed house was to be built. Although the trials were undertaken in calm weather, their success proved that operating a lifeboat and launching from the site would

The first production 13m Shannon, carrying no name her but subsequently being christened Jock and Annie Slater, exercising with Andy Pearce in April 2013. Andy Pearce launched so that some of the crew could see the boat at first hand and undertake familiarisation with the new design and, in particular, her jet-drive propulsion. (Alun Pari Huws)

Lifeboat official number 1325 under construction at the ALC, Poole, April 2016. The purpose-built facility constructed six Shannon class lifeboats a year, and the boat for Llandudno was the eighteenth Shannon to be constructed. The start of the lay-up of the hull was on 20 April 2015, fit-out started on 8 March 2016, the boat was launched on 16 November 2016, with a proving trial on 5 December 2016 and hull and equipment trial on 10 January 2017, prior to acceptance on 11 January 2017. (Nicholas Leach)

be possible in all weathers, with several launchings and recoveries being undertaken at different states of the tide.

By the time construction of the new station had started in the spring of 2016, a further coast review in January 2016 confirmed the decision that a new Shannon class lifeboat would be sent to the station. In preparation for this, the first production Shannon, *Jock and Annie Slater* from the Relief Fleet, had visited Llandudno in 2013 and an exercise with *Andy Pearce* had been undertaken to give crew some experience on board the new class of lifeboat.

The new boathouse was built by local firm Wynne Construction, and it was finally completed in June 2017, being taken over by the RNLI the following month. The site at Craig-y-Don proved to be a better long-term solution than any of the other schemes. During the twenty years that efforts had been made to find a new boathouse, there had been a significant increase in traffic in the busy town, especially in the summer months, but the new house was more convenient to reach for many of the crew, and the facilities were

William F. Yates at the RNLI College, Poole, September 2017, prior to coming to station. (Nicholas Leach)

Relief 13m Shannon Cosandra at Craig-y-Don during launch and recovery training, July 2017. Coxswain Graham Heritage (above) was on board during the training, the main aim of which was for the shore crew to become familiar with the SLRS rig, which was completely diffrent from the Talus MB-H. (EFAS)

The brand new 13m Shannon William F. Yates is lowered into the water for the first time at the All-Weather Lifeboat Centre at Poole, following her completion. (RNLI)

fit for modern life-saving operations. The launch directly across the beach also meant that launch times were greatly reduced.

In 2015 confirmation was received regarding the new Shannon lifeboat with official number 1325, with the operational number 13-18, being allocated to the station. The boat was to be named *William F. Yates* at the request of the principal donor, Gladys Yates, in memory of her late husband. Mrs Yates died in 2001, but had stipulated that the money be used for a lifeboat at Llandudno so it had been held since then to honour the terms of her bequest. Mr and Mrs Yates had retired to Llandudno many years previously close to where the new boathouse was eventually built.

William F. Yates was built at the RNLI's in-house boatbuilding facility in Poole. Work on the new boat commenced in early 2016 and the completed craft was placed in the water for the first time on 15 November 2016. Trials were conducted during the latter part of November and into December 2016, but with the boathouse at Llandudno far from complete, the boat was kept in storage in Poole until the building was ready. With a completion date of late June 2017 for the new boathouse, training schedules were organised,

On board William F. Yates at the RNLI College, Poole before heading to North Wales are, left to right, Tim James, Luke Heritage, Graham Heritage, Les Jones and Mike Jones. (By courtesy of Llandudno RNLI)

The passage crew on board William F. Yates at Conwy just before the lifeboat was taken to Llandudno for the first time are, left to right, Les Jones (Mechanic), Mike Jones, Graham Heritage (Coxswain), Tim James (Second Coxswain) Luke Heritage and Andrew McHaffie (Fleet Staff Coxswain). (By courtesy of Llandudno RNLI)

William F. Yates, escorted by Conwy ILB D-765 May-Bob, arrives at Conwy on 23 September 2017 during her passage from Poole to North Wales. The passage to station saw the boat call at Brixham on 20 September, Newlyn on 21 September, and Kilmore Quay on 22 September, before she reached Conwy. (By courtesy of Llandudno RNLI)

William F. Yates arrives at Llandudno on 24 September 2017, being escorted round the bay by 12m Mersey Andy Pearce, with D class inflatable Dr Barbara Saunderson (D-793) also on hand to join with the celebrations. (Nicholas Leach)

William F. Yates arriving at Llandudno on 24 September 2017, and showing her speed as she passes the lifeboat house at Craig-y-Don, where hundreds of supporters had gathered to welcome the new boat. (Nicholas Leach)

starting with a course for SLRS operators on the beach using relief rig SC-T02. In July 2017 relief Shannon *Cosandra* came to the station for a few days and a series of launch and recovery trials were undertaken to enable the shore crew to become familiar with the SLRS rig designed to launch and recover the Shannon lifeboat.

In early June 2017 four of the station's five Coxswains went to Poole for an intensive week working on the RNLI's training boats, as well as the station's own new boat. In late July Assistant Coxswain/Assistant Mechanic Danny James, Assistant Mechanic Les Howell and crew members Phil Howell and Bert Williams travelled to Poole for familiarisation aboard the new station boat. Staff Coxswain Andrew McHaffie was in command, supported by trainer Paul Rogers. During the familiarisation training, and while she was on passage from Newhaven to Poole via the Solent on 23 July 2017, *William F.Yates* was asked to help search for a speedboat which was disabled in the Solent; the boat was duly located and

William F. Yates is brought into the new lifeboat house for the first time, 23 September 2017, with the SLRS rig SC-T14 hauling her inside. (Nicholas Leach)

towed to Portsmouth harbour, its three occupants unharmed. Later that day, while returning to Poole harbour, *William F. Yates* was asked by Poole Harbour Control to assist a 25ft motor sailing vessel, which had become disabled in the main shipping channel. The crew quickly secured a towline to bring the vessel to safety, before returning to the RNLI's base.

In early September 2017 Mechanic Les Jones, with three of the station's five assistant mechanics, went to Poole for an intensive course on Shannon machinery. Shortly after their return, the station's new SLRS unit arrived, direct from the manufacturer, Biglands of Montgomery, with preparations for the arrival of the new boat being stepped up.

Llandudno's passage crew travelled to Poole on Sunday 17 September 2017 and between 18 and 20 September completed pre-passage preparations. On board for the passage were Coxswain Graham Heritage, Mechanic Les Jones, Second Coxswain Tim James and crew members Luke Heritage and Mike Jones. On 20 September the boat started its first leg of the passage home, under

William F. Yates being launched at Craig-y-Don during launch and recovery training on 28 September 2017. During the day, the lifeboat was launched and recovered several times as the crew and shore team learned about the launching procedure. (Nicholas Leach)

William F. Yates being recovered during launch and recovery training on 28 September 2017 prior to the new lifeboat being placed on station. (Nicholas Leach)

Relief 12m Shannon Cosandra was at Llandudno for the week after the arrival of station boat William F. Yates to assist with crew training and familiarisation, and was involved in launch and recovery training on 28 September 2017. (Nicholas Leach)

William F. Yates and Relief 12m Shannon Cosandra being launched during launch and recovery training on 28 September 2017. (Nicholas Leach)

Below: William F. Yates and Cosandra together off Llandudno during crew training, 28 September 2017. (Nicholas Leach)

the command of Fleet Staff Coxswain Andrew McHaffie, travelling from Poole to Brixham. On 21 September they went to Newlyn, and the following day from Newlyn to Kilmore Quay. On 23 September the boat and her crew left Kilmore Quay and headed across the Irish Sea to Conwy. Newlyn to Kilmore Quay was a long passage and the provided the crew with their first real experience of operating the boat in moderate to rough conditions.

There was unexpected drama during the final leg from Kilmore Quay to Conwy. As *William F. Yates* was rounding Carmel Head on Anglesey's north-western tip, the crew was alerted to the launch of both Moelfre and Beaumaris lifeboats assisting a 23m motor yacht, which had struck rocks near Moelfre and was taking in water. Moelfre lifeboat towed the boat to safer inshore waters but the water ingress was so great that even pumps from both lifeboats could not stem the flow. By now, *William F. Yates* had rounded Point Lynas at the north-eastern tip of the island and was making good speed to provide assistance which had been requested by Holyhead Coastguard. The crew of *William F. Yates* put their pump aboard

D class inflatable D-793 Dr Barbara Saunderson was placed on station on 6 April 2016, and is pictured being launched on exercise just over a month later. (Nicholas Leach)

D class inflatable D-793 Dr Barbara Saunderson on exercise off the pier on 14 May 2016. D-793 was the third inshore lifeboat at the station to be funded by the late Dr Barbara Saunderson. She was named and dedicated on 21 October 2017. (Nicholas Leach)

The naming ceremony of William F. Yates took place on 21 October 2017, when Storm Brian was passing over, meaning the event was held inside the new lifeboat house. (Nicholas Leach)

and with the additional pump the water ingress was slowed and the vessel was towed to Beaumaris to be beached. *William F. Yates* was released in time for her to make the tidal gate at Conwy Marina.

On 22 September 2017 the relief Shannon *Cosandra*, which had been at station for SLRS training during the summer, arrived at Conwy Marina and the following day a number of crew undertook Shannon familiarisation aboard the boat. Many of the crew were present to greet *William F. Yates* when she arrived at Conwy at the end of eventful final leg of her passage to North Wales.

The long awaited new lifeboat arrived at her new home on Sunday 24 September 2017. *Andy Pearce* and D class inflatable

The naming ceremony of William F. Yates took place on 21 October 2017, with the lifeboat being launched in the teeth of Storm Brian and guests braving the strong winds and torrential rain to witness the boat being put through her paces. Coxswain Graham Heritage poured the champagne over the lifeboat's bow (above), with the wind taking it away. (Nicholas Leach)

Barbara Saunderson were launched soon after 11am and met *William F. Yates* off Pen Trwyn at the Orme's Head, where a number of boats and jet skis were also on hand to provide an escort. At midday the boats entered the bay, sweeping in towards the pier first and then making their way along the bay to the new boathouse at Craig-y-Don, where a crowd of more than 1,000 well-wishers and supporters had gathered. After showing her capabilities and giving time for the crew of *Andy Pearce* to moor that lifeboat, *William F. Yates* was beached for the first time at around 12.45pm to the applause of the crowd. She was then recovered onto the SLRS rig, and brought into the new boathouse, her home.

Ray Evans (1940-2015) former Deputy Launching Authority, who championed the cause for a new lifeboat house at Llandudno for almost twenty years.

With the Shannon in situ, intensive crew training began the following day and continued until the following Sunday. During the weekend of 7 and 8 October 2017 the crew were passed out by the RNLI's Shannon implementation team, who declared themselves very satisfied with the performance of the volunteers and the lifeboat was formally declared operational at 9am on 10 October 2017.

The naming ceremony for the new lifeboat took place on 21 October 2017, when not only was the new Shannon christened but the SLARS rig was accepted, the new boathouse was formally opened and the D class inshore lifeboat D-793 *Dr Barbara Saunderson* was named in what was a unique ceremony. The initial plans for the ceremony were made with fair weather in mind, with a large crowd expected outside as well as the formally invited guests. However, it proved to be challenging weather, with Storm Brian crossing the country and bringing torrential rain and strong winds, which only a few supporters braved.

The ceremony started at 1pm under the stewardship of Dr J.J. Green, the station's long-serving Medical Advisor and, latterly,

Mechanic Les Jones, left, and Coxswain Graham Heritage, right, lead the crew and shore helpers through the town for the last launch of Andy Pearce. The RNLI's standard bearer that day was Gareth Parry, Deputy Launching Authority and former helm at Beaumaris station. Watched by hundreds of supporters and well-wishers, the lifeboat was brought through the streets for the last time on 18 November 2017 to be launched at the North Shore. (By courtesy of Llandudno RNLI)

Chairman. The boathouse was formally opened by Michael Vlasto, former Operations Director of the RNLI, and Jenny Evans, widow of the late Ray Evans, former Deputy Launching Authority who had worked tirelessly over almost twenty years for a new boathouse in Llandudno. Michael Vlasto was well known to many of the longer-serving volunteers from his time as District Inspector in Wales. The Rev Beverley Ramsden, minister at St David's Methodist Church, Craig-y-Don, officiated at the service of dedication.

Both lifeboats and SLRS launching rig were formally accepted on behalf of the RNLI by George Rawlinson, Operations Director and also well known to station personnel, who in turn handed them to the care of the station. Captain Marcus Elliott, long-serving Lifeboat Operations Manager, accepted the lifeboats on behalf of the station. The inshore lifeboat was named *Dr Barbara Saunderson* by the donor's brother, Brian, and *William F. Yates* was named by Peter Forster-Dean, executor of the late Gladys Yates' estate, with Rev Noel Carter, Rector of Llanrhos-Cystennin and Canon Phillip Barratt, Station Chaplain officiating.

Andy Pearce, watched by hundreds of supporters and well-wishers, is launched for the last time at Llandudno, 18 November 2017.
(Phil Griffiths)

Andy Pearce after her last launch, with the new lifeboat house at Craig-y-Don in the background. (Phil Griffiths)

Andy Pearce arrives at Conwy, escorted by Conwy ILB D-765 May-Bob, 18 November 2017. (Phil Griffiths)

It was expected that Rescue 936, the MCA Coastguard helicopter based at Caernarfon, would make a brief appearance at the end of the ceremony while the lifeboats were being prepared for launch. However, winds of fifty-five knots and driving rain put paid to this. *William F. Yates* was launched in the pouring rain, watching by more than 100 people braving the conditions to see the boat in action, but D class ILB *Dr Barbara Saunderson* did not put to sea as dumping surf had built up on the shoreline. It was a memorable day which gave many guests, donors and supporters an opportunity to see lifeboat and shore crews go about their work undeterred by the conditions.

Andy Pearce out of the water at Pwllheli in December 2017 prior to taking up her first relief duty in January 2018. (Dan Jones)

William F. Yates' first call came soon after the naming ceremony, on 8 November 2017, when she was tasked at 11.58pm to help a 8m fishing craft which had broken down in Conwy Bay. Although conditions were fair, it was blowing force five to six and Conwy ILB was also tasked. The new lifeboat launched at 12.17am and reached the casualty in half an hour. After towing the boat to the Conwy

In March 2018 Graham Heritage (left) and Les Jones received awards from the RNLI to recognise their dedicated service as members of the town's lifeboat crew for over thirty years. Graham first volunteered in 1986 and has worked his way up, first to Assistant Mechanic, then Second Coxswain, before being appointed as Coxswain in 2011. Les first volunteered for the crew in early 1986, working his way up to Assistant Mechanic before being appointed to his present post as full-time Mechanic in 1999.

river and handing it over to Conwy ILB to secure the vessel, the crew of *William F. Yates* returned to station at 3.30am.

William F. Yates' second call came on 4 December 2017, when she was called out at 5.50pm with Rhyl lifeboat *Lil Cunningham* by Holyhead Coastguard to go to the assistance of the windfarm support vessel *Kitty Petra*, which had reported a fire on board. The casualty, with three persons on board, was close to the south-eastern boundary of Gwynt-y-Mor windfarm, and her mayday broadcast had resulted in other craft in the vicinity going to help, while both lifeboats made full speed to the scene. In the event, the casualty's situation was brought under control unaided so *Kitty Petra* was able to make slow progress towards the Port of Mostyn, escorted by Rhyl lifeboat. Llandudno lifeboat was released at 6.55pm to return to station.

In between the two services, the emotional last launch of 12m Mersey *Andy Pearce* took place on 18 November 2017. Most of the volunteer crew and shore helpers were on hand to walk ahead of the lifeboat as she made a last journey down Lloyd Street from the boathouse which had been her home for twenty-seven years, during which time she had been involved in more than 300 rescues and helped save fifty lives. Coxswain Graham Heritage, one of the crew who brought *Andy Pearce* to Llandudno in 1990, said the day was tinged with 'pride and sadness'. Lifeboat Operations Manager, Marcus Elliott, said the departure 'marks the end of an era' as it was the last time an all-weather lifeboat was towed through the streets to be launched, bringing an end to the 156-years-old practice. Hundreds of people walked with the lifeboat down to the Promenade, and watched the final launch from the North Shore. After putting to sea with Coxswain Heritage at the wheel, *Andy Pearce* circled round the bay for one last time and then headed for Conwy Marina. She was placed in the RNLI's Relief Fleet, undertaking a first relief duty at Pwllheli.

13m Shannon lifeboat William F. Yates and D class inflatable Dr Barbara Saunderson on exercise off Llandudno, March 2018. (Nicholas Leach)

Rough weather exercise launch of William F. Yates on 18 March 2018. (Dennis Oliver)

Llandudno lifeboat station 2017: 13m Shannon William F. Yates outside the new lifeboat house, with inshore lifeboat D-793 Dr Barbara Saunderson and Bobcat BC09, the vehcile used to flatten the shingle on the beach as well as launch the ILB. (Nicholas Leach)

Meanwhile, public interest in the new boathouse and lifeboat was considerable. Many individuals and groups were given tours of the new facility, but with operations taking priority following the naming ceremony, the station was not able to receive visitors or members of the public until the end of 2017. The boathouse was formally opened to public viewing between Christmas and new year 2017, and hundreds of people were welcomed during a three-day period. They were able to see at first hand the new facilities, the impressive new lifeboat and appreciate the dedication of the volunteers who are on call twenty-four hours a day, as they have been since the station was established in 1861.

William F. Yates being washed down outside the lifeboat house after an exercise, and made ready for service. (Nicholas Leach)

Inshore lifeboats at Conwy

T he picturesque town of Conwy, dominated by a magnificent castle built by Edward I in 1284, lies a few miles west of Llandudno. In medieval times it was a major port, and since the 1960s has been a popular holiday resort, with visitors coming to enjoy its shops, walk the historic town walls, and of course visit the castle. For more than half a century the town has been home to an inshore lifeboat station, which was established at more or less the same time as the inshore lifeboat (ILB) came to Llandudno. The introduction of small fast, manoeuvrable inflatable lifeboats to the RNLI fleet came in 1963 in response to an increasing number of incidents involving yachts, dinghies and other small pleasure craft, as well as swimmers and bathers. They were intended for inshore rescue work and in the mid-1960s one was allocated to Conwy. In June 1966 the first ILB, No.97, was placed on service, just a year after Llandudno had received an

The picturesque town of Conwy, with the medieval walls encircling most of the houses, and the first ILB house just visible on the quay to the far left of this photograph.

ILB, and a small, somewhat basic boathouse was built beneath the castle walls, on the quay. The ILB was launched by trolley into the estuary, to go upriver or out to sea as required. The boat's arrival was celebrated in style, with the Mayor going out in the inflatable for a spin during the inaugural launch event on 9 June 1966.

Conwy's sphere of operations extends from the Great Orme's Head to the north, westward to Dutchman's Bank and up the Conwy river towards the village of Trefriw and, very occasionally, beyond. The area overlaps with neighbouring lifeboat stations at Beaumaris (to the west) and Llandudno (to the east), and the

A visit to Conwy in 1967 by Lt Cdr Harold Harvey, RNLI Inspector for No.8 Lifeboat Area, to check on the station's inshore rescue boat, No.97, with some of the volunteer crew in attendance. (John Lawson Reay, by courtesy of the RNLI)

The first inshore rescue boat at Conwy, No.97, taking the Mayor out during the inaugural celebrations on 9 June 1966. (By courtesy of Conwy RNLI)

ILB crews have often worked with colleagues from these stations. Navigation in and around the estuary is greatly dependent on tidal conditions. With over 1,400 craft using the river and its adjoining marinas, traffic can be dense and there are hazards for mariners and those on the shore, particularly muddy ground, with spring tides running at over seven knots at their fiercest making conditions particularly challenging. This makes navigation into and out of Conwy, while routine in fair conditions, dangerous in bad weather.

The first services performed by IRB No.97 came during the late summer of 1966, a couple of months after the boat had arrived, with three incidents attended by the newly-enrolled volunteers in the space of three days. On 5 August a speedboat was brought in after its sole occupant fell overboard, and the following day the body of a missing person was landed. On 7 August the ILB and her crew landed five people after they had got cut off by the tide, and on 16 and 17 August two small boats were helped, respectively the yacht *Hazard* and the motor cruiser *Maranita*.

On 30 August 1970 the Conwy IRB crew undertook a particularly fine service, when the cabin cruiser *Fulmar* got into difficulty off the West Shore at Llandudno in heavy broken seas. Three hours after high water the honorary secretary was informed by the police that a boat was in difficulties, a mile west of the Great Orme. The IRB was launched, with the crew facing south-westerly force five to six winds, causing heavy broken seas at the Great Orme. The IRB left harbour at 2pm and headed for the reported position of the casualty, using the deepwater channel

Conwy's first inshore rescue
boat D-97 being launched
on service at 2.05pm on
6 June 1967 to the yacht
Ebb Tide, which had broken
down off Penmaenmawr.
(Photos by Jeff Morris)

Inshore rescue boat D-97 returning from service to the yacht Ebb Tide, which had broken down, bringing the owner to safety, 6 June 1967. (Photos by Jeff Morris)

The four rescued crew from the yacht Ebb Tide walking up the jetty at Conwy after the RAF rescue helicopter had taken them off the yacht Ebb Tide, 6 June 1967. (Photos by Jeff Morris)

Inshore rescue boat D-97 being brought ashore following the service to the yacht Ebb Tide, 6 June 1967. (Photos by Jeff Morris)

Conwy's first lifeboat volunteers: K. Bar, I. Lomas, M. Mason, D. Smith, T. Price, Keith Robinson, R. Craven, J. Roberts, K. Rimmer, F. Smith, Trevor Jones, D. Jones, Lt Cdr Harold Harvey (RNLI Divisional Inspector) and J. Williams. (By courtesy of Conwy RNLI)

parallel to the West Shore, and ending up passing the casualty, which was at anchor. When nothing was found at the reported position, it was realised what had happened, and on returning the IRB crew found that the 30ft motor cruiser, with two men on board, had a rope round her propeller and a damaged gearbox.

In view of the big seas running, the IRB crew decided it would not be practicable to try and tow the casualty to safety, so the two men were taken off. Two runs alongside had to be made to allow the men to jump aboard the IRB. The survivors were totally exhausted when they were landed at Conwy, while their cruiser became a total loss in the next day. It was reported that the service was carried out in very bad conditions in shallow water with some

The first IRB house was a somewht rudimentary garage with space for the IRB on her trolley, and the basic protective gear hanging on the walls. Crew facilities were virtually non-existent. (By courtesy of the RNLI)

danger to the crew and no chance of other assistance. Helmsman Brian Jones, Ronald Craven and Trevor Jones were accorded the Thanks Inscribed on Vellum by the RNLI in recognition of the courage they showed in the rescue of two men.

Brian Jones (on helm) and Desmond Craven (bow) on Conwy's first IRB No.97. (By courtesy of the RNLI)

New ILB during the 1970s

In August 1971 a new inshore lifeboat (ILB), as inshore rescue boats were designated in the early 1970s, was sent to Conwy. The new ILB was a 15ft 3in Zodiac Mk.II type, number D-205, and she served the station for almost five years. She was replaced in March 1976 by D-239, another Zodiac Mk.II type, which had been funded by the Wodensburgh High School in Wednesbury, West Midlands. This ILB remained on station for more than a decade, and was involved in a fine service just over a year after she arrived.

On 14 April 1977 a motor fishing vessel went ashore on the south side of the Conwy approach channel. The station's deputy launching authority was alerted to the vessel's plight by Penmon Coastguard at 7.52am. The maroons were fired and at 8.10am the ILB was launched, setting out for Deganwy Point at full speed and battling a north-westerly strong to near gale force six to seven wind which was causing short, steep, breaking swell in the harbour entrance. On reaching Deganwy Point, the ILB helmsman reduced speed because of the swell, and the casualty was sighted aground on the Morfa Mussel Bank about 200 yards south-west of Perch Light, listing to port, with seas breaking over her starboard quarter. The ILB crew also saw someone standing on her deck.

Helmsman Trevor Jones took the ILB alongside and secured her under the lee of the casualty's port bow at 8.15am. The vessel was on passage from Amlwch to Conwy and had anchored in the

D-205, the station's second ILB, on exercise with a Wessex helicopter from RAF Valley in the early 1970s. (By courtesy of Conwy RNLI)

approach channel because gearbox trouble had left her without propulsion. Her anchor cable had parted and she had been blown ashore. At the request of the skipper, the ILB ran a line ashore, securing the boat by a wire hawser to a large rock above high water mark, before taking off the crew and landing them at Conwy Quay at 8.50am. The ILB was rehoused and made ready for service by 9.15am. For this fine service, letters of appreciation, signed by Captain Nigel Dixon, RN, Director of the Institution, were sent to Helmsman Jones and crew member F. Smith.

On Saturday 19 January 1980 two young girls, Mandy Warren and Katie Flowers, were walking near Benarth Point on Conwy Estuary when, at about 9.15am, they heard shouts for help in the distance and shots being fired. They ran to the shore and saw a

D-97, Conwy's first inshore lifeboat, served from June 1966 to August 1971. (By courtesy of Conwy RNLI)

man trapped on the mud bank by the rising spring tide, which was coming in fast. Realising the danger he was in, Mandy remained on the shore to keep him in sight, while Katie ran to the nearest telephone to raise the alarm.

On receiving the call, Conwy Police immediately informed the DLA, who fired the maroons. The crew assembled within minutes and the D class inflatable was launched at 9.20am. Reaching the man a few minutes later, Helmsman John F. Smith and crew member Trevor Jones found him trapped chest high in mud with the flood tide rapidly rising. He was pulled out of the mud and brought ashore by the ILB, which was rehoused and made ready for service at 9.40am. The man had been out wild-fowling on the estuary mud flats and been trapped in an extremely dangerous area of deep soft mud gullies, some of which are 9ft deep. But for the prompt and correct action of the two girls, he might have lost his life and letters of appreciation, signed by Cdr Bruce Cairns, RNLI Chief of Operations, were sent to those involved in this rescue.

In 1985 a new ILB house was built on the Quay, close to the road bridge, on the same site as the previous small garage, which had been used since the station was opened. The more sturdy and larger building, erected on a site adjacent to the Harbour Office, was formally opened on 20 July 1985 by the Mayor of Conwy, S.R. Roberts, and two years later, in 1987, a new ILB was sent to the station. The 16ft 3in Avon EA16 type inflatable D-346 *Yachting Monthly* had been funded through an appeal by Yachting Monthly magazine, and was the first of the station's ILB to be given a name. On 30 April 1988 a handing-over ceremony and service

D-239 outside the ILB house.
(By courtesy of Conwy RNLI)

of dedication was held at the station, during which Andrew Bray, Editor of Yachting Monthly, formally delivered the ILB into the care of the RNLI, being accepted by Honorary Secretary Keith Robinson. After a short service of dedication conducted by the Rev Canon Dwyfor Jones, the new ILB was launched for a quick demonstration of her capabilities.

D-346 *Yachting Monthly* was one of several inshore lifeboats on the North Wales coast called to help with relief work when floods hit the Llandudno area on 10 and 11 June 1993. D class ILBs and volunteer crew also came from Llandudno, Rhyl and Flint, with some making long journeys by road. Although it had been quite severely flooded, Llandudno's boathouse became the local Coastguard operation's centre as it still had an operational VHF radio, telephone and heating, which was more than the Coastguard's building nearby. All four stations received letters from the RNLI's Chief of Operations recognising their efforts.

Conwy's D class inflatable was towed to the flooded area at 6.45pm and evacuated numerous people, returning for essential medication and to check the still-live electric power substations, before being stood down at 2am. Llandudno's ILB was in the thick of the flooded area and the crew using their boat were able to help 180 people to safety over the course of two days. Flint's ILB was under way by 9.40pm, making the forty-mile passage to Llandudno by road towed by Land Rover. Boat, vehicle and crew helped people from the water to places of safety untl being stood down during the early hours of 11 June.

On 21 June 1995 a new D class inflatable was placed on station. D-482 *Arthur Bate* was funded from the bequest of the late Arthur

Honorary Secretary Keith Robinson accepting the keys of the second ILB house from the Mayor of Conwy, Captain S.R. Roberts, who formally declared the building open at the end of a special ceremony on 20 July 1985. (By courtesy of Conwy RNLI)

The second ILB house on the Quay was built in 1985 and was larger than the house it replaced, on the same site. It was formally handed over and dedicated at ceremony on 20 July 1985. It is pictured in September 1989 (top), September 1994 (centre right) and November 1996 (bottom), with different signage above the main doors. (Nicholas Leach)

At the naming ceremony of D-346 are, from left to right, Gwyn Craven, Ricky Fryer, John Owen, Michael Hughes, Robin Hughes and Trevor Jones. (By courtesy of Conwy RNLI)

Charles Bate and the boat was handed over during a ceremony held at the lifeboat station on 9 September 1995, attended by a large number of people. The new ILB was formally presented to the RNLI by Miss Joan Bate, sister of the late donor, and she was accepted by Lt Cdr Brian Miles, Director of the RNLI who in turn passed her into the care of Honorary Secretary Keith Robinson. After a service of dedication by the Rev Peter Jones, Miss Bate formally christened the new ILB.

In 2000 a new and larger ILB house was built and extended to provide improved crew facilities and housing for the ILB. The new boathouse was considerably larger than the previous ILB houses, with a first floor crew room and a small souvenir shop incorporated into the building. The boathall was large enough to accommodate

An aerial view of Conwy Quay, showing the second ILB house beneath the medieval town walls. (By courtesy of the RNLI)

a launch vehicle, which speeded up launch times. The construction of the new building was part of the RNLI's long-term plans to provide modern shore facilities around the coast.

On 18 August 2004 the station's next new inshore lifeboat, D-627 *Arthur Bate II,* was placed on station. She was a new type of ILB, known as the IB1, and had a 50hp outboard engine, more powerful and faster than her predecessor, with a speed of twenty-five knots, and she was fitted with a standardised 'pod' in the bow containing all the necessary equipment. She was funded, like her predecessor, from the bequest of the late Arthur Charles Bate, and the naming ceremony took place on 13 November 2004, in bright winter sunshine. During the ceremony, Roger Fellows and Shirley Hadley, executors of Arthur's sister Miss Joan Bate,

D-482 Arthur Bate on exercise in the estuary. (Nicholas Leach)

The ILB house built in 2000 providing improved crew facilities and housing for the ILB, with a first floor crew room and a small souvenir shop. When it was first built (top photo, seen in August 2000), the launchway was not in line with the boathouse doors. (Nicholas Leach)

The ILB house built in 2000, pictued in 2012 after a new launchway had been built from the Quay into the river. (Nicholas Leach)

D-482 Arthur Bate inside the ILB house. The main doors of the boathouse are often opened so that passers-by can see the ILB and make a donation in the collection box. (Nicholas Leach)

D-482 Arthur Bate on her launching trolley outside the ILB house. When the station was first established, the ILB was pushed into the water by hand, with the Honda Quadbike later provided to make launching easier. (Nicholas Leach)

handed over the ILB into the care of the RNLI. Andy Hurley, RNLI Training Inspector West Division, passed her into the care of the station and she was formally accepted by honorary secretary Keith Robinson. The Rev Canon Peter Jones conducted the service of dedication, after which Clifford Hadley named the ILB.

After ten years in service, D-627 was replaced by a new ILB, D-765 *The May-Bob*, which became the seventh ILB to serve at Conwy. The new ILB arrived on 19 March 2014 and was named on 18 August 2014 when, despite it being summer time, brollies were needed as the station's supporters gathered for the ceremony, although the rain failed to dampen the enthusiasm of supporters who gathered for the occasion. The new £41,000 ILB was funded by Mavis (May) Kane, who wanted to help the RNLI before she passed away. By donating funds from both her estate and that of her father, Bob, she was able to help towards the cost of the new ILB.

Mavis Kane was born and raised in Liverpool and worked for most of her life in the city. She took early retirement and bought a

Lifeboat volunteers and station pesonnel during the naming ceremony of D-627 Arthur Bate II on 13 November 2004. (Nicholas Leach)

D-627 Arthur Bate II puts out at the end of her naming ceremony on 13 November 2004. (Nicholas Leach)

property near Holywell. She passed away in 2000 at the age of sixty-three. Her nephew, David Brown, handed over the lifeboat to the RNLI and named the lifeboat in memory of Mavis (May) and her father. The new ILB had launched nineteen times and rescued thirty-one people between entering service and the naming ceremony. Canon G. Berw Hughes led the service of dedication and Maelgwn Male Voice Choir led guests in hymns and the Welsh and English national anthems. RNLI Regional Operations Manager Colin Williams accepted the lifeboat on behalf of the RNLI and handed her into the care of the station.

Within a year of arriving the new ILB was involved in a fine service after a person fell into the water as he was transferring

D-627 Arthur Bate II being recovered after her naming ceremony on 13 November 2004. (Nicholas Leach)

D-765 The May-Bob flies the flag as she is put through her paces after her naming ceremony on 18 August 2014. (Nicholas Leach)

The scene during the naming ceremony of D-765 The May-Bob at Conwy Quay on 18 August 2014. Standing in front of the new ILB are Greg Donald, Patrick Byrnes, Clare Roberts and Scott Hughes. (Nicholas Leach)

from the vessel to a pontoon on 15 January 2015. The incident was captured on the headcam of one of the volunteers and was widely seen on television, giving the station considerable publicity as it showed vividly how the crew quickly located the casualty, seventy-year-old David Stocks, rushed to his aid, and saved his life. The Llandudno pensioner spent twelve minutes in freezing cold water after falling into the River Conwy, quickly drifting out to sea with the tide. But he managed to grab hold of a boat and just managed to stay afloat until help arrived.

Fortunately, some of the lifeboat volunteers were working nearby when the call for help came, and crew members Greg Donald, Pete Hughes and Alan Flood launched the ILB within four minutes of the alarm being raised. In the extremely cold temperatures, David was barely conscious when the ILB arrived on scene. Alan Flood immediately entered the water to help keep David afloat, while the other two crew pulled him into the ILB. The lifeboat then sped back to shore to a waiting ambulance, which took him to hospital for further treatment as he was in danger of post-rescue collapse. David said afterwards: 'They were just brilliant and kept talking to me and asking me about my grandkids to keep me conscious. Apart from a few bruises, I'm alive and this incident really does put things into perspective.'

D-765 The May-Bob is put through her paces off the Quay after her naming ceremony on 18 August 2014. (Nicholas Leach)

David Stocks with two of his rescuers: Conwy lifeboat crew Greg Donald (left) and Peter Hughes (right). (By courtesy of the RNLI)

Conwy lifeboat crew celebrating the 50th anniversary of the station; standing in front of the D class inflatable The May-Bob (D-765) are, left to right, Peter Hughes and Trevor Jones (former LOM); in the ILB are Michael Thomas, Danny-Lee Davies and Alan Flood. (Danielle Rush/RNLI)

In 2016 the station celebrated the remarkable achievement of half a century of service. On 18 June the crew gathered at Conwy Comrades Club for a dinner to mark the anniversary with the focus being on seventy-one-year-old Trevor Jones, who had been involved from the start and thus received a well-deserved award. Trevor was aged just twenty-two when he signed up at the station and went on to save 166 lives. He recalled the early years in the 1960s and 1970s: 'In those days we were all fisherman who worked around the quay. There was a lot of lads eager to join the lifeboat, but I'm the only one still left for one reason or another.'

The work of lifesaving continued and on 30 January 2017 D-765 *The May-Bob* was launched at 11.45am to assist a 33ft yacht which had suffered engine failure in Conwy Bay. Once on scene, an ILB crew member was able to board the yacht and assist the lone skipper, rigging a tow and bringing the yacht into the river. A side tow had to be set up for the passage back into Conwy due to the strong tidal conditions, and the ILB safely towed the yacht back to her swinging mooring outside the lifeboat station. The lifeboat arrived back on station at 12.40pm, where she was recovered,

D-765 The May-Bob on exercise in the River Conwy, crewed by Danny-Lee Davies (on helm), Gavin Chamberlain and Michael Thomas. (Nicholas Leach)

D-765 The May-Bob heads out of Conwy on exercise crewed by Danny-Lee Davies on the helm, Gavin Chamberlain and Michael Thomas. As well as covering the Conwy estuary and shores in the vicinity, Conwy ILB covers Llandudno's West Shore together with Llandudno's ILB, depending on the state of the tide and location of a casualty. The two stations have a fine history of working together particularly when, for example, larger boats are in difficulty and an all-weather boat is required to support the ILBs. (Nicholas Leach)

Conwy and Llandudno ILBs exercising together: D-765 The May-Bob and D-793 Dr Barbara Saunderson (on right) in the Conwy Estuary. (Nicholas Leach)

Above: D-765 The May-Bob being recovered using the New Holland TC31 tractor TA76, which has been in service since 1976. (Nicholas Leach)

Right: Gavin Chamberlain, Danny-Lee Davies and Michael Thomas with the ILB on the Quay. (Nicholas Leach)

refuelled and made ready for service. This was the third callout for the volunteer crew in January, which is usually a very quiet month.

On 11 March 2017 *The May-Bob* launched at 2.35pm shortly after concerns were raised about the occupants of a vessel stranded in an isolated location. Once the ILB was near the casualty, it was ascertained that the occupants had lifejackets and were happy to stay with the vessel until the next high tide. The ILB made her way back through the shallows of the river back to the LB house, where she was recovered. She was relaunched at 8.10pm to provide safety cover and illumination while the vessel refloated in case of the hull was damaged. At 9.10pm the vessel successfully refloated and, in a strong flood tide, was escorted safely back to Conwy Marina.

The lifeboat station at Llanddulas

Midway between Abergele and Colwyn Bay lies the village of Llanddulas, from where a lifeboat was operated for more than sixty years. The beach at Llanddulas, close by Penmaen Head, was once a steep one of shingle and is exposed to northerly winds. Llanddulas is perhaps best known for its limestone quarries, which were worked for more than 200 years. The first jetty for the shipment of stone was built in 1822, enabling vessels to come in on the tide and lie alongside to load. Others were built later, and a busy coastal traffic scene developed between Llanddulas and Lancashire ports, most of which were situated on the Mersey. The railway that runs through the village, and along the North Wales coast linking Holyhead – and thus Dublin – to London dates from the 1840s.

The lifeboat station was founded during the same era as that at Llandudno, but its establishment was somewhat unusual. In the late 1860s the RNLI was considering placing another lifeboat on the coast of North Wales. Of the locations under consideration, Abergele, five miles west of Rhyl, was initially chosen. According to *The Lifeboat* of 1 July 1869, 'it was considered desirable to

Looking over the beach, bathing huts and lifeboat house seen from the railway. Llanddulas railway station was opened on 1 July 1889 by the London and North Western Railway, and was served by what is now the North Wales Coast Line between Chester and Holyhead. The line was built by the Chester and Holyhead Railway during the 1840s. (By courtesy of Brian Bell)

View from Railway, Llanddulas.

have another lifeboat in this locality, worked by the same crew as that which managed the Rhyl Tubular Life-boat, and under the control of the Local Committee at Rhyl. Wrecks frequently occurred in the neighbourhood which could not be reached by the Rhyl Lifeboat without much delay.' A self-righting lifeboat, measuring 33ft by 8ft 6in and rowing ten oars, was built, along with a transporting carriage, and the intention was to establish a station at Abergele.

Named *Henry Nixson No.2*, the lifeboat was forwarded to North Wales in January 1868, but never went to Abergele. It 'temporarily occupied the place of the [Rhyl] tubular lifeboat', which was being repaired in Liverpool, being kept in the old lifeboat house at Foryd, to the west of Rhyl, until a decision had been made about the most suitable site for a permanent lifeboat house, but as Llanddulas was deemed a more suitable location, being centrally placed between the two existing stations at Rhyl and Llandudno, Abergele was never opened. So, soon after the boat intended for Abergele reached Rhyl, it was moved to Llanddulas. *The Lifeboat* of 1 January 1870 reported: 'Llanddulas has been chosen as the most eligible spot, the people of the neighbourhood being also most anxious to have the boat, and there being an excellent site available for a lifeboat house, a good beach for launching, and a competent crew to work the boat.'

Henry Nixson No.2 was one of the fourteen lifeboats presented to the RNLI by the Manchester Branch, and was named after the man who had given the money, and who had, four years earlier, funded a lifeboat for Maryport, which was named *Henry Nixon No.1*. R.B. Hesketh, of Gwrych Castle (a nineteenth century country house near Abergele), presented the site for the boathouse, and also funded the entire cost of its construction. The new station was publicly inaugurated on 25 September 1869, when the lifeboat was taken from Foryd, being drawn by six horses loaned by William Owen, of the Bee Hotel, Abergele, and met at Tan-yr-Ogof by a procession formed with the band of the Denbigh Volunteers leading the committee and the village school children. The lifeboat followed at the rear of the procession, with the thirteen crew and two Coastguards on board, with oars upright. On arrival at the beach, after 'an appropriate prayer had been offered up by the Rev J. Davies, the Honorary Secretary to the Llanddulas Branch', as *The Lifeboat* reported, the lifeboat was launched for a demonstration.

The boathouse built on the beach cost £150, and the site was used throughout the station's life. Provision of a crew was a minor problem, as there was no port or haven, and so no seamen or fishermen. But from the local quarrymen, those who worked on the stone jetties, retired seamen in the village and the Coastguards, sufficient men could be mustered when needed.

The Llanddulas Railway Bridge was destroyed by floods on 17 August 1879, but was soon rebuilt. Photographs of the damage also show the original lifeboat house of 1869. (By courtesy of Brian Bell)

Debris from the destroyed railway viaduct being removed on 26 August 1879. The temporary railway line over the wooden bridge is complete and in use, and the original lifeboat house to the right, with bathing huts in the background. (Bob Rawcliffe's collection)

It was seven years before *Henry Nixson No.2* was first called upon. Then, on 30 July 1876, she was launched to a small vessel in distress about a mile offshore, and she soon reached the casualty, the pleasure boat *Eagle*, of Llandudno, with the lifeboat crew finding five people on board, who were all exhausted. They were taken on board the lifeboat and brought ashore at Llanddulas. *Eagle* had lost her mast, was half full of water, and was in danger of sinking.

Two more services were undertaken by *Henry Nixson No.2* during her sixteen years on station. The first, on 19 January 1877, was to the smack *Ann Pritchard*, of Caernarfon, which had been seen flying a signal of distress three miles from the station in south-westerly gale-force winds. After the lifeboat volunteers had pulled at the lifeboat's oars for an hour and a half, the smack was reached and boarded. She had parted from her anchor cable, was leaking badly and was unmanageable, and the two persons on board had given themselves up for lost. The lifeboat crew not only saved the two men, but also managed to run their vessel onto the beach to save her, before the lifeboat returned to station.

The second Llanddulas lifeboat, the 34ft self-righter Mary Jane Gould, on her carriage on the beach outside the lifeboat house.

The other service occurred seven years later, on the morning of 14 May 1884, when seven men were saved from the Norwegian brigantine *St Olaf*, of Mandal. The brigantine was laden with pit props and was bound for Connah's Quay when she capsized about three miles out at sea off Llanddulas. Her crew of six and a pilot took to the ship's boat. The casualty was soon reported at the lifeboat station, so *Henry Nixson No.2* put out at 8.40am, and proceeded to their aid. The shipwrecked men were taken onto the lifeboat and landed at Foryd, near Rhyl. The ship's boat would almost certainly have foundered had not the lifeboat reached it, as a westerly gale was blowing, accompanied by rough seas.

In the years between these services two vessels were wrecked at Llanddulas. In 1880 the flat *John and Mary*, while waiting to load at one of the jetties, was caught out in worsening weather conditions and went ashore; her crew of two were saved without the help of the lifeboat. The other wreck was that of the schooner *Helca*, in a north-westerly gale, in 1882. There was concern at the time that the Llanddulas lifeboat had not been launched to help, and the

Mary Jane Gould on her carriage outside the lifeboat house, circa 1890. The tall man in the centre, with baggy white sleeves and arms hanging down, is Richard Roberts, coxswain from 1886 to 1911. His graveyard is in the churchyard of St Cynbryd's Parish Church, Llanddulas. (Bob Rawcliffe's collection, courtesy of Brian Bell)

local committee held an inquiry into the matter, which one of the RNLI Inspectors attended. However, the inquiry exonerated the coxswain and crew for not launching in the prevailing conditions.

In 1885 *Henry Nixson No.2* was withdrawn from service and replaced by a new self-righter, which was larger than her predecessor, measuring 34ft by 8ft 3in, and built by Forrestt at Limehouse. She provided more stability, but her greater weight made the launch and recovery process over the loose shingle on the beach more difficult. She was one of two new lifeboats funded from a generous legacy, received through the Manchester Branch, from the estate of the late John Gould, of Didsbury, Lancashire. The first of the

William Williams (on right) and his family; he was awarded a Silver medal for gallantry by the RNLI for the rescue of Ocean Queen on 7 November 1890. (By courtesy of Brian Bell)

two boats went to Llanddwyn in Anglesey and was named *Richard Henry Gould*, while the second came to Llanddulas and was named *Mary Jane Gould*. She arrived at Llanddulas in April 1885 and on 4 May was taken afloat in rough seas and strong north-easterly wind, after which, according to *The Lifeboat*, 'the coxswain and crew . . . reported highly of her behaviour in rough water, stating that they liked her very much, and considered her a better Boat, and more suitable for the requirements of the station, than her predecessor'.

During the twenty-four years this lifeboat served at Llanddulas, demand for her services was minimal. Apart from exercise launches, she launched only three times on service. Two of the three services were undertaken in 1888, on both occasions to small Liverpool-registered steam coasters employed in the quarry trade being the casualties. The first was on the morning of 6 October 1888, when the steamship *Tolfaen*, bound from Liverpool for Newry, was seen at anchor in Rhos Bay, with a heavy list to port and flying signals of distress in a strong north-westerly gale and very heavy seas.

Mary Jane Gould was immediately taken out of her house, horses were procured, and the boat was conveyed by road to Llandrillo, five miles away, as the wind and sea were unfavourable for launching at Llanddulas. The journey was quickly accomplished, and the lifeboat was launched. When she and her crew arrived on scene, it was found that five of the crew of seven men had been lost in the storm in the early morning when the steamer was about ten

The 34ft self-righter Mary Jane Gould on the beach with her crew and station personnel. Built in 1885 by Forrestt, Mary Jane Gould was on station from April 1885 to 1909. (Bob Rawcliffe's collection)

miles north-east of the Great Orme's Head; they had taken to their boat, or were preparing to board it, thinking the steamer would sink after her cargo shifted, when the boat and men were washed away. Only the master and fireman were left on board, but they managed to bring the steamer into Rhos Bay, and dropped anchor. Some of the lifeboat crew boarded the vessel, and she was taken to Garth, in the Menai Strait, where she arrived in the afternoon.

The other service was a month later, on 6 November 1888, when *Mary Jane Gould* put off to help the steam flat *Widnes*, of Liverpool, which showed a signal of distress in a strong south-easterly breeze and rough seas while at anchor off Llanddulas. When they reached the vessel, the lifeboat crew found that she was leaking badly, and so, at the request of the master, some of the lifeboat crew went on board to assist at the pumps, and take the steamer to the relative safety of the Menai Strait.

The third and final service of *Mary Jane Gould* was on 10 January 1890 to the yacht *Blue Rock*, of New Brighton, which was in difficulty opposite Beach House. The lifeboat put out at 10.05am into heavy seas and, on reaching the yacht, the lifeboat crew found only one occupant, her owner, on board; he was on passage from New Brighton to Conwy, so he was quickly taken on board the lifeboat and safely landed ashore.

As well as the lifeboat undertaking rescues, some excellent rescues were effected by shore boats during this period, including one by Second Coxswain Richard Roberts, when he saved the crew of the Runcorn flat Dido, which was stranded at Penmaenrhos in a strong gale and very heavy seas on 8 January 1886. For his gallantry, he was awarded the RNLI's Silver medal and the Board of Trade Bronze medal, and the RNLI also granted £1 to each of the other thirteen men who helped.

At 9am on 7 November 1890, after a night of severe winds, the schooner *Ocean Queen* was seen labouring heavily out to sea off Llanddulas, her top-sails flying in shreds. She appeared completely out of control and drifted across, going ashore on the rocks below the quarries at Penmaen Head. The seas were breaking over her decks and the four crew had to shelter in the rigging. The schooner was not fast aground, however, but was rolling heavily as she finally came to rest about 150 yards offshore in a mass of broken water. The onlookers who had gathered anxiously to await the arrival of the lifeboat, which was housed about a mile or so to the east, saw no sign of it arriving, so some quarrymen procured a small boat and carried it to a point opposite the wreck.

Four of them volunteered to try and reach the schooner, and between them got the boat afloat. They pulled hard at the oars, but each time they got afloat their boat was hurled ashore by the breakers. Two more attempts were made by a different group, but these also failed, and the men were fortunate not to be drowned. There was still no sign of the lifeboat and it was decided to telegraph to Llandudno asking for help from there. The Llandudno crew was already out on service, however, and so another attempt was made to launch the small boat. Undaunted by two more unsuccessful attempts, the men persisted and on the sixth attempt managed to get the boat beyond the first line of massive breakers without being upset and thrown back. The schooner's crew of four were thus saved, but were exhausted when they were got ashore.

Meanwhile, as all this was happening, the lifeboat crew and a few helpers had made repeated attempts to launch *Mary Jane Gould*. Most of the local populace had gone to the scene of the wreck and there were probably not enough for the task of getting the

Mary Jane Gould being launched from her carriage, with the crew holding oars raised and at the ready. (Bob Rawcliffe's collection, courtesy of Brian Bell)

heavy boat to the water across the shingle. Once there, conditions in the onshore gale were atrocious and attempts to get afloat were unsuccessful. The only alternative left was to obtain horses and haul the lifeboat by road and along the beach to a point near the wreck in the hope of being able to launch there. They asked nearby farms to supply horses and were getting a team together when some of the spectators came back and told them of the rescue of the schooner's crew. The greatest credit was due to the rescuers, who had persevered against great odds and achieved what seemed to be almost impossible. The four men who accomplished this rescue were John Roberts, quarryman, second coxswain of the lifeboat; John Jones, quarryman; William Williams, quarryman; and William Williams, shopkeeper. For this extremely dangerous and gallant act, the four men were awarded the Silver medal by the RNLI, as well as the Royal Humane Society's medal.

On 10 November 1896 the schooner *Jameson*, bound from Liverpool to Conwy with timber, was wrecked off Colwyn Bay in a northerly gale and heavy rain, and at 9pm the crew burned signals of distress. Messages were sent to both the Llanddulas and the Llandudno stations. The former's crew were mustered but again had extreme difficulty in attempting to launch and eventually abandoned any hope of getting off, facing enormous seas breaking on the exposed shore. The distressed vessel was, meanwhile, drifting nearer the coast and eventually struck below the embankment of the railway between Old Colwyn and the entrance to Llysfaen tunnel. One of her crew later recounted that they had left Liverpool about 10am in a fair south-easterly wind, which later veered to the north and increased in force.

They saw the lights of Llandudno and, realising that they could not weather the Orme, the master altered course to try and haul off the lee shore. The gale relentlessly drove his vessel closer to the shore, and so he let go both anchors to try and stop her.

The lifeboat crew wearing cork lifejackets, circa 1903. John Davies, honorary secretary from 1890 to 1907, is on the far right, standing next to the chairman, the Rev C.F. Roberts. (Bob Rawcliffe's collection, courtesy of Brian Bell)

The scene during the inaugural launch of the station's last lifeboat, Brother and Sister, on 9 October 1909, when hundreds of people from the surrounding district assembled to witness the proceedings. The lifeboat was named by the Countess of Dundonald. The carriage is fitted with Tipping's plates, which were first used at the station in January 1892. (Bob Rawcliffe's collection, courtesy of Brian Bell)

Both cables soon parted and, with her masts gone and bulwarks stoved in, she went ashore. A number of local residents, attracted by the signals of distress in the blackness of the night, gathered on the shore and did everything they could to rescue the crew. The master and one seaman were dragged ashore through the surf without injury, but were exhausted from their exertions. Another of the crew had been flung with such violence by a wave against the broken bulwarks when the schooner was ashore that both his legs were badly fractured. He was dragged ashore in great pain and, although rushed to hospital, died shortly afterwards. The final member of the crew was missing and on the Sunday morning, when the tide had ebbed, the wreck was examined and his body was found jammed beneath timbers torn from the hull.

After this tragic incident, efforts were made by a number of Colwyn Bay residents to have a lifeboat stationed there. A request was sent to the RNLI in London, but after consideration the idea was rejected by the national organisation. The proposal was discussed

Brother and Sister on the beach, on her carriage, probably after recovery. During her twenty-three years on station she launched four times on service and is credited with saving six lives. (Bob Rawcliffe's collection, courtesy of Brian Bell)

over a period of time, and was finally abandoned in June 1901.

In 1906, while on exercise off Llanddulas, *Mary Jane Gould* was struck by a heavy sea and thrown on her beam ends. Six men who were holding a warp were thrown overboard and the second coxswain, Robert Jones, sustained a broken leg. Fortunately none of the six men were lost, but Jones was disabled for more than ten months and received £85 16s 4d in compensation.

The following year, 1907, new arrangements were made for the supply of horses to be used for launching, a flat rate of 10s being agreed irrespective of whether they were called in summer or winter, and whether by day or night. This, it was hoped, would greatly improve launching at the station, which had been a persistent problem. A local casualty in October of that same year was the small steamer *Cameo*, which had just completed loading

Brother and Sister beaching in 1922, possibly following what proved to be the last service undertaken by the station's lifeboats, on 19 September to the schooner Chevalier Bayard, of St Malo. (Bob Rawcliffe's collection, courtesy of Brian Bell)

stone at one of the jetties when a sudden squall drove her broadside on to the beach. Her cargo had to be unloaded before she could be refloated.

Almost twenty years had passed since *Mary Jane Gould's* last service when she was replaced in 1909 by a Liverpool type sailing lifeboat. This boat, longer, heavier and more powerful than the self-righter, was built by the Thames Iron Works at Blackwall, London, at a cost of £939 4s 0d. She measured 36ft by 9ft, carried twelve oars and was fitted with two water-ballast tanks and two drop keels. The total weight of the boat, when ready to be put to sea, was three tons seventeen hundredweight, with the iron keel weighing eleven hundredweight. With her tanks full,

and crew of fifteen on board, she drew 1ft 10in of water, and was described in *The Lifeboat* as being 'the very latest type, . . . a very fine sea boat, excellent in every way and was unequalled along the coast'. The lifeboat house was altered to accommodate the new lifeboat, at a cost of approximately £430, with the extension being built on land owned by the Countess of Dundonald.

During the afternoon of Saturday 9 October 1909 the inauguration ceremony for the new lifeboat was held. She had been funded from the legacy of the late Miss Louisa B. Courtenay, of Brompton Square, London, and was named *Brother and Sister*. Before the ceremony, hundreds of people from the surrounding district had assembled, and the Llanddulas Silver Band performed a variety of music. Lieut E.D. Drury, RNR, the RNLI's Inspector of the Western District, represented the RNLI. The Countess of Dundonald, accompanied by Lady Marjory Cochrane and the

Lfieboat day at Llanddulas, with the Brother and Sister lifeboat on her carriage being drawn through the village; wearing the bowler hat, standing centre near the horse's head, is George Roberts. (Bob Rawcliffe's collection, courtesy of Brian Bell)

A team of seven horses was used to launch the lifeboat at Llandulas, here pulling the station's last lifeboat, Brother and Sister, in 1909.

Two of the coxswains, William Williams (1923-30, on left) and John Jones (1911-23, centre), with Edward Jones (on right) outside the lifeboat house, in front of Brother and Sister during the latter days of the station's existence.

Hon Robin Cochrane, arrived by motor car, and was shown over the lifeboat by Lieut Drury, with the Rev Dr Hall presiding over the formalities of the ceremony. Lieut Drury handed the boat into the care of the local committee, and reminded the attendees that Lady Dundonald's father, more than forty years ago, had named the first Llanddulas lifeboat. The Chairman then called for three cheers for her Ladyship, and, after Canon Roberts had read a prayer, the Countess named the boat, breaking a flask of wine against her bows, and saying 'God speed and good luck to the Brother and Sister'. The boat was launched for a demonstration, and undertook a short trip with her sails hoisted for the benefit of the onlookers.

Her first launch by *Brother and Sister*, on 9 January 1910, saw her rescue six men from the Irish schooner *Gwalia*, of Drogheda, off Startled Fawn beach. The schooner, bound from Liverpool with coal, was observed in the Bay showing signals of distress shortly before noon, so the crew were summoned, and although they were 'mostly in their different places of worship', as *The Lifeboat's*

A proposal was made to station a lifeboat at Colwyn Bay in the 1890s, but the only lifeboat Colwyn Bay was to receive was the former Point of Ayr lifeboat H. G. Powell, which was sent there for exhibition purposes, being displayed on the promenade in 1916. (From an old postcard supplied by John Harrop)

account explained, the lifeboat was quickly launched. In the teeth of a westerly gale, she was rowed to the sinking vessel from which the entire crew were rescued and brought ashore, 'amid much excitement amongst the large crowd assembled on the beach'. The sea was extremely rough, and the schooner subsequently stranded.

There was a long gap before another service was effected, suggesting that the station's usefulness was coming to an end. This time assistance was rendered to the French schooner *Chevalier Bayard*, of St Malo, which was in difficulty about four miles

The lifeboat house pictured in August 1954, twenty-two years after the station closed. (Grahame Farr, by courtesy of the RNLI)

The original service boards are mounted inside the boathouse. (Nicholas Leach)

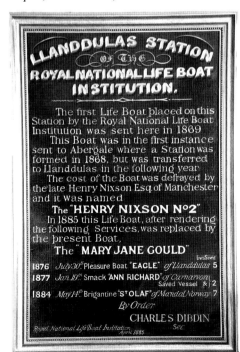

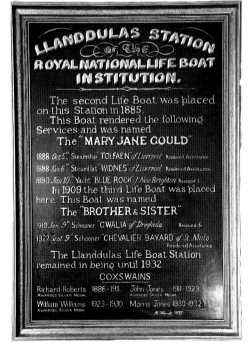

The lifeboat house built in 1869 and altered in 1909 was used throughout the life of the station, and has been converted into a private residence known as 'The Old Lifeboat House', with a large extension on the eastern side. The house was built with walls of local limestone 2ft 3in thick, and was publicly inaugurated on 25 September 1869. The alterations of 1909 involved an extension towards the railway embankment so that a new and larger lifeboat, 36ft long, could be accommodated. The building was sold when the station was closed in December 1932, and in about 1955 Vincent and Margaret Worrall and family moved into, and modified, the extension on the east side which had been built, but not lived in, by the previous owner. The Worralls later converted the boathouse itself into living accommodation, and added a double garage in 1981. In February 1996 the property was bought by the present owners, Brian and Vi Bell. The beach no longer slopes gently down from the Old Lifeboat House to the sea. The ground has been built up to be horizontal as part of the sea defences, before dropping further out to the sloping beach. (Nicholas Leach)

north-east of the boathouse on 19 September 1922. The Coxswain was keeping an eye on the vessel and, as the weather worsened during the evening, the lifeboat put out at 6.30pm. The vessel was bound for France, but although her six crew were French and could speak no English, the lifeboat crew soon found that she was helpless with her sails damaged. The lifeboat crew organised for a tug to attend, and returned to station at 11.15pm.

In the next decade, with no further services undertaken, the RNLI Committee decided, at a meeting on 13 October 1932, that a station was no longer necessary at Llanddulas. New motor lifeboats were due at Llandudno and Rhyl, and these could cover the area more speedily and effectively. Thus, Llanddulas station was closed in December 1932, with *Brother and Sister* being sold out of service locally. The station had not been busy at any period in its history, and there were always problems with launching from the open shingle beach, which afforded no shelter whatsoever from onshore gales. During the sixty-four years of the station's existence, just fifteen launches took place and twenty-one lives saved.

Appendices

A • Lifeboat summary

Years on station (launches/saved)	Dimensions Type	Cost ON	Year built Builder	Name Donor
1.1861 – 1867 (7/8)	32' x 7'10" Self-righting	£190 —	1860 Forrestt	Sisters Memorial Gift of the Misses Brown, Liverpool
7.1867 – 1887 (16/35)	33' x 8'7" Self-righting	£246 —	1867 Forrestt	Sisters Memorial Gift of the Misses Browne, Liverpool
10.1887 – 1902 (19/26)	37' x 8' Self-righting	£529 124	1887 Forrestt	Sunlight No.1 Lever Bros, Warrington
7.1902 – 1930 (42/39)	37' x 9'3" Self-righting	£908 486	1902 Thames IW	Theodore Price Legacy of Miss A.G.G. Rolleston, London
6.1930 – 1931 (3/0)	37' x 9'3" Self-righting	£911 465	1901 Thames IW	Sarah Jane Turner Gift of Sir Samuel Turner, Rochdale
1931 – 1933 (1/0)	37' x 9'3" Self-righting	£928 512	1903 Thames IW	Matthew Simpson Gift of Misses Simpson, Lancaster
1933 – 1953 (57/38)	35'6"x 9'3" Self-righting (M)	£3,010 768	1933 J.S. White	Thomas and Annie Wade Richards Legacy of Dr Thomas Richards, augmented by the late Miss Sarah Lewis, Aberystwyth
1953 – 1959 (17/8)	35'6" x 10'8" Self-righting (M)	£10,573 851	1947 J.S. White	Tillie Morrison, Sheffield Gift from James and David Morrison
6.1959 – 1.1964 (36/21)	35'6" x 10'3" Liverpool (M)	£3,771 792	1936 J.S. White	Annie Ronald and Isabella Forrest Gift of Miss A. Ronald, legacy of Mrs I. Forrest.
1.1964 – 11.1990 (116/58)	37' x 11'6" Oakley	£33,000 976	1964 Groves & Guttridge	Lilly Wainwright Legacy of W.H. Wainwright, York, gift from Arthur Jowett Fund and RNLI Funds
11.1990 – 10.2017	38' x 12'6" Mersey	£429,494 1164	1990 FBM Ltd	Andy Pearce Bequests of Andrew Pearce and Ralph Merriott
10.2017 –	13m Shannon	£2,000,000 1325	2017 ALC, Poole	William F. Yates Bequest of Mrs Gladys Yates, with other donors

Llandudno's longest-serving pulling lifeboat Theodore Price, on her carriage in November 1923 for the visit to the town of HRH Prince of Wales, later King Edward VIII. (By courtesy of Llandudno RNLI)

B • Inshore lifeboats summary

Years on station (launches/saved)	ON	Name (if any) Donor	Type Notes
5.1965 – 10.1966	D-54	— —	15'3" RFD PB16
3.1967 – 10.1976	D-109	*James* Gift of Mrs S.J. Sutcliffe and her sister Miss M.A. Law.	15'3" RFD PB16
3.1977 – 1988	D-250	— Green Shield Trading Stamps Appeal in Tesco.	Zodiac Mk.II
1988 – 10.1996	D-359	*41 Club I* The Association of ex-Tablers Clubs (41 Club).	16'6" Avon EA16
2.10.1996 – 11.2006	D-508	*John Saunderson* Gift of Dr Barbara Saunderson, Llanfairfechan.	16'6" Avon EA16
21.11.2006 – 4.2016	D-656	*William Robert Saunderson* Gift of Dr Barbara Saunderson, Llanfairfechan.	IB1
6.4.2016 –	D-793	*Dr Barbara Saunderson* Gift of Dr Barbara Saunderson, Llanfairfechan.	IB1

D class inflatable D-793 Dr Barbara Saunderson is the seventh ILB to serve at Llandudno. (Nicholas Leach)

C • Launching vehicles

Years on station	ON	Type
1933 –	T33	Clayton
27.7.1948 – 56	T40	Case LA1
1956 – 1961	T31	Case type L
1961 – 1964	T33	Case type L
1964 – 1965	T73	Case 1000D
1965 – 1969	T72	Case 1000
10.1969 – 1977	T56	Fowler Challenger III
12.1977 – 1987	T86	Case 1150B
9.1987 – 1999	T102	Talus MB-H
1999 – 2008	T94	Talus MB-H
2008 – 2017	T91	Talus MB-H
2017 –	SC-T14	SLRS Supacat

Relief SLRS tractor unit SC-T02 during trials, July 2017.

D • Motor lifeboat details

Thomas and Annie Wade Richards

Official Number	768
On station	Sep 1933 – Feb 1953
Record	57 launches, 38 lives saved
Dimensions	35'6" x 9'3"
Type	Self-righting motor
Engines	Single 35bhp Weyburn petrol engine
Weight	5 tons 16 cwt
Built	J.S. White, Cowes
Donor	Legacy of Dr Thomas Richards, Llangadoch, augmented by a legacy of the late Miss Sarah Lewis, Aberystwyth
Cost	£3,010 0d 7d
Notes	Named on 28.9.1934 by Miss A.E. Lewis
Disposal	Sold 3.1953 for £360 to Mr H. Evans, Criccieth, for use s a fishing boat at Aberystwyth and Rhyl, renamed *Craiglais*, then *Wil Ifan* and finally *Dolphin*; by the 1990s she was at Coburg Dock, Liverpool, and was believed to have been broken up at Tranmere in 2003-04

Tillie Morrison, Sheffield

Official Number	851
On station	Feb 1953 – Sep 1959
Record	17 launches, 8 lives saved
Dimensions	35'6" x 10'
Type	Self-righting motor
Engines	Twin 18bhp Weyburn AE4 petrol engines
Weight	7 tons 15 cwt
Built	1947, J.S. White, Cowes
Donor	Gift from James and David Morrison, of Sheffield, in memory of their sister
Cost	£10,573 5s 9d
Notes	Named on 8.5.1948 at Bridlington by HRH Duchess of Kent
Disposal	Sold 11.1959 for £525 to Leslie Shaw, of Manchester, and converted into a fishing boat at Rhyl and then Newcastle, where she was renamed *Imishi*; by 2012 she was at Hartlepool, renamed *Elizabeth*; in 2014 she was moved to North Wales by Ships' Timbers Maritime Museum, Llandudno, and was taken to Deganwy Quay Marina, opposite Conwy, to be restored for possible display

Annie Ronald and Isabella Forrest

Official Number	792
On station	Jun 1959 – Jan 1964
Record	36 launches, 21 lives saved
Dimensions	35'6" x 10'3"
Type	Liverpool motor
Engines	Single 35bhp Weyburn AE6
Weight	6 tons 4 cwt
Built	1936, J.S. White, Cowes
Donor	Gift of Miss A. Ronald and legacy of Mrs I. Forrest
Cost	£3,770 19s 6d
Notes	Named on 12.7.1937 at St Abbs by Lady Jean Graham; stationed at St Abbs 1936-49, Reserve 1949-56 and Scarborough 1956-58
Diposal	Sold 13.7.1965 for £1,255 to A.W. Webb, Solihull; renamed *Petomi* and used as a pleasure boat in Essex; she was renamed *Ocean Wanderer*, and ended up ashore in a storage yard at Walton-on-the-Naze

Thomas and Annie Wade Richards going off her carriage and burying her bow. She was powered by a single 35bhp Weyburn petrol engine driving a single propeller, which can just be seen in a protective tunnel at the stern. (By courtesy of Llandudno RNLI)

Lily Wainwright on display on the Promenade, 28 May 1968. Her engine casing is painted grey and she has not had the operational number, 37-09, added. She was powered by twin 52hp Parsons Porbeagle diesels. (Jeff Morris)

13m Shannon William F. Yates on exercise, 29 March 2018. She is powered by two 650hp Scania D13 diesel engines, coupled to twin Hamilton HJ364 waterjets, giving a speed of over twenty-five knots. (Nicholas Leach)

Lilly Wainwright

Official Number	976, operational number 37-09
On station	Jan 1964 – Nov 1990
Record	116 launches, 58 lives saved
Dimensions	37' x 11'6"
Type	Oakley
Engines	Twin 52hp Parsons Porbeagle diesels
Weight	12 tons 8 cwt
Built	1964, Groves and Guttridge, Cowes
Donor	Legacy of Mr Wainwright, gift from the Arthur Jowett Fund and RNLI Funds
Cost	£32,230 11s 6d
Notes	Named on 15.5.1964 by HRH Princess Marina, Duchess of Kent
Disposal	Sold 1.10.1993 to Cobh Heritage Trust, and stored at Cobh, Co Cork, for many years, unconverted and unaltered; in 2016, after a long and sympathetic refit, including moving the engines to the survivor space, she was relaunched for use as a pleasure craft based at Rushbrooke and East Ferry, Cork, Ireland

Andy Pearce

Official Number	1164, operational number 12-006
On station	23 Nov 1990 – Oct 2017
Record	249 launches, 50 lives saved
Dimensions	11.6m x 4m
Type	Mersey, aluminium hull
Engines	Twin 285hp Caterpillar 3208T diesels
Weight	14 tons
Built	1990, FBM Ltd, Cowes
Donor	Bequests of Andrew Stephen Pearce and Ralph C. Merriott, together with other gifts and legacies
Cost	£429,494.70
Notes	Named on 18.6.1991 by HRH The Duchess of Kent

Willliam F. Yates

Official Number	1325, operational number 13-18
On station	Oct 2017 –
Dimensions	13m x 4.4m
Type	Shannon
Engines	Twin 13-litre Scania D13 650hp engines, driving twin Hamilton HJ364 waterjets
Weight	18 tons
Built	2017, All-Weather Lifeboat Centre, Poole
Donor	Bequest of Mrs Gladys Yates, in memory of William Frederick Marple Yates, of Widnes, together with other gifts and legacies
Cost	£2 million
Notes	Named on 21.10.2017 by Peter Forster-Dean

E • Service summary

The Sisters Memorial Lifeboat

1861   Sep 13   Smack *Uncle Tom*, of Runcorn, rendered assistance
1864   Dec 7   Flat *Morning Star*, of Carnarvon, saved vessel and 3
1866   Feb 27   Flat *Morning Star*, of Carnarvon, saved 3
     Dec 7   Smack *Cymro*, of Amlwch, saved vessel and 2

The Sisters Memorial (second) Lifeboat

1867   Sep 20   Smack *Jane*, of Carnarvon, assisted to save vessel and 4
1869   Nov 4   Netherlands brigantine *Catherina*, saved 5
1870   Oct 13   Steamship *Fox*, of Middlesbrough, rendered assistance
1872   Oct 10   Flat *Swallow*, of Runcorn, saved 3
     11   Brigantine *Coila*, arranged for steam tug
     16   Flat *Peter*, of Liverpool, saved 4
1875   Jan 1   Flat *Esther*, of Beaumaris, saved 2
1877   Dec 24   Steamship *King Ja-Ja*, of Carnarvon, saved 10
1881   Nov 22   Smack *Ellen*, of Beaumaris, saved abandoned vessel
1884   Apr 28   Yacht *Wave*, of Liverpool, saved 3
1885   Oct 10   Sailing boat *Mira*, of Llandudno, saved boat and 4
1887   Sep 7   Yacht *Haidee*, of Liverpool, saved yacht's boat

Sunlight No.1 Lifeboat

1889   Oct 7   Fishing smack *Perseverance*, of Liverpool, saved 4
     Fishing smack *Ellen and Ann*, of Douglas, saved 4
1890   Nov 7   Schooner *Planet*, of Carnarvon, saved 5
1892   Feb 1   Schooner *John Nelson*, of Beaumaris, saved 2
     Ketch *Sea Gull*, of Beaumaris, saved 3
1893   Dec 8   Barque *Eivion*, of Carnarvon, rendered assistance
1894   Dec 22   Ketch trawler *Scotian*, of Liverpool, saved 4
1896   Apr 12   Brigantine *Warree*, of Dundalk, saved 4
1897   Sep 2   Schooner *Dora*, of Chester, saved abandoned vessel

Theodore Price Lifeboat

1903   Feb 1   Steamship *Wylam*, of Limerick, stood by and landed 1
     19   Smack *Stag*, of Beaumaris, saved 2
1904   Feb 12   Schooner *Progress*, of Wicklow, beached derelict vessel
1906   Dec 12   Schooner *Lorne*, of Aberystwyth, saved (also a dog) 2
1907   Sep 2   Smack *Midsummer*, of Douglas, saved 1
1908   Sep 9   Schooner *Fanny*, of Beaumaris, rendered assistance

1910   Jan 1   Fishing boat *Adela*, of Llandudno, saved boat and 2
     July 6   Smack *Hero*, of Rhyl, saved 2
1911   Oct 30   Schooner *Jane and Ann*, of Carnarvon, rendered assistance
1912   Aug 4   Cutter yacht *Muriel*, of Liverpool, saved 4
     Oct 18-9   Fishing boat *Primrose*, of Llandudno, saved boat and 2
1914   Aug 10   Pleasure boats *Dylis* and *Annie*, of Llandudno, saved boats and 10
     Dec 8   Fishing boat *Nellie*, of Llandudno, rendered assistance (saved boat and 3)
1919   Mar 27   Schooner *Ada Mary*, of Liverpool, saved 2
1920   Jan 8   Schooner *Dundarg*, of Padstow, saved 5
     11   Schooner *Jane and Ann*, of Carnarvon, landed 4
     Schooner Dundarg, of Padstow, landed 5
1922   Dec 21   Rowing boat *White Lily*, of Llandudno, saved boat and 2
1923   Oct 29   Fishing boat *Alice*, of Llandudno, saved boat and 2
     Two drifting boats, saved boats
1927   Oct 22   Motor yacht *Delphore*, of Liverpool, saved 3

Sarah Jane Turner Lifeboat

1931   July 18   Yacht *Frosette*, of West Kirby, stood by and escorted

Thomas and Annie Wade Richards Lifeboat

1934   May 6   Yacht *Mizpah*, of Liverpool, saved yacht and 3
     Aug 20   Yacht *Mizpah*, of Liverpool, saved yacht and 3
1935   Oct 18   Fishing boat *Barbara*, of Llandudno, saved boat and 3
1936   Aug 7   Yacht *Mona*, of Heswall, landed 3
1939   June 2   HM Submarine *Thetis*, took a doctor to HMS *Somali*
1940   Aug 31   Rowing boat *Shamrock*, of Colwyn Bay, saved boat and 2
     Nov 9   Steam trawler *Leonard*, of Fleetwood, assisted to save vessel
1942   Dec 1   Fishing boat *Margaret*, of Conwy, stood by
1943   Jan 27   Motor fishing boat *Pilot III*, and rowing boat *Eira*, of Llandudno, saved boats and 6
     31   Man fallen over cliff, picked up a body
     Apr 25   Fishing boat *Dorothy*, of Llandudno, saved boat and 3
1944   Jan 7   North Western lightvessel, took out provisions
     June 5   Man over cliffs, landed a body
     Aug 27   Rowing boat *Dawn*, of Colwyn Bay, saved 2

1945	June 20	Motor fishing boat *Clarissa*, of Bideford, landed 2
1946	July 30	Fishing boat, saved boat and 2
	Aug 29	Fishing boat *Delia*, saved boat and 2
	Sep 27	Two dinghies, saved dinghies and 2
1947	Jan 21	North Western lightvessel and lightship tender *Watchful*, took out a doctor and landed injured man
	Apr 6	Yacht *Sark*, saved yacht and 5
	Nov 15	Yacht *The Witch*, of Conwy, escorted
1948	Sep 15	Fishing boat *Yap*, of Conwy, escorted
1952	Jan 8	Motor vessel *Benwood*, of Liverpool, esc'd
	Apr 10	Fishing boat *Liver Bird*, of Conwy, saved boat and 1

Tillie Morrison, Sheffield Lifeboat

1953	June 1	Motor boat from HMS *Verulam*, gave help and landed 12
	Dec 13	Three rowing boats, escorted
1954	Oct 23	Fishing boat *Amorosa*, of Rhyl, escorted
1957	May 12	Three canoes, escorted
	Sep 7	Two dinghies, saved 4
	9	Yacht *Tricia*, of Liverpool, stood by
1958	July 26	Yacht *Thebe*, of Wallasey, saved yacht and 2
	Sep 27	Rowing boat, saved boat and 2

Annie Ronald and Isabella Forrest Lifeboat

1959	Oct 4	Speedboat *Airess*, saved boat and 2
		Rowing boat, saved boat and 4
1960	July 21	Sailing dinghy, escorted
1961	Mar 11	Dinghy, saved dinghy
	June 17	Dinghy, landed 2
	July 2	Three rowing boats and a motor boat, gave help
	9	Sailing dinghy *Shian*, saved dinghy
	Aug 19	Boat, saved boat
1962	Mar 19	Dinghy, saved dinghy
	May 29	Boy fallen over cliff, gave help
	June 14	Sailing dinghy, saved dinghy
	Aug 9	Yacht *Hazhad*, saved boat (also a dog) and 4
	14	Man trapped by tide, saved 1
		Motor launch and six yachts, saved boats and 5
	Oct 21	Canoe and rowing boat, gave help

Frank and William Oates Reserve Lifeboat

| 1963 | Apr 14 | Cabin cruiser *June*, gave help and landed 3 |

Annie Ronald and Isabella Forrest Lifeboat

1963	June 22	Fishing boat *Christina*, of Rhyl, saved boat and 5
	Aug 5	Motor launch towing cruiser, escorted and gave help
	20	Small yacht, gave help
	Sep 7	Three yachts, saved one yacht and gave help to two yacht

Lilly Wainwright Lifeboat

1964	Mar 13	Sailing dinghy, saved dinghy
	May 3	Cabin cruiser *Almeria*, took out doctor, saved yacht and 4
	24	Man stranded on rocks, saved 2
	Aug 23	Yacht *Marie II*, saved yacht and 3
1965	Apr 16	Sailing dinghy *Wix*, of Penmaenmawr, saved dinghy and 3
	May 15	Cabin cruiser *Westwind*, saved cruiser and 3
	June 30	Yacht *Cormorant*, saved yacht and 2
	July 11	Speedboats and motor boat, gave help
1966	Apr 11	Sailing dinghy, saved dinghy and 3
	May 21	Yachts, saved two yachts
	Aug 4	Motor vessel *Emereld*, of Glasgow, landed an injured man
1967	July 29	Cruiser *Anita Mar*, gave help
	Oct 1	Motor yacht, saved yacht
	Dec 8	Motor vessel *Farringay*, of Cardiff, assisted to save vessel
1968	Mar 26	Fishing boat *CO.359*, of Carnarvon, and its punt, saved boats and 2
	May 6	Cabin cruiser *Calypso*, of Wallasey, saved cruiser and 5
		Motor vessel *St Trillo*, of Liverpool, gave help
	Aug 12	Trimaran *Lady of the Isles*, gave help
	17	Sailing dinghies, gave help
1969	July 21	Trawler *Southern Isle*, took out doctor and landed a body
	Sep 21	Dinghy, saved dinghy and 2
		Three dinghies, saved three dinghies
1970	Apr 12	Cabin cruiser *Shemara*, escorted
	July 12	Cabin cruiser *Ellen*, in tow of motor fishing boat Silver Star, gave help
	Sep 13	Motor boat *Evelyn*, saved boat and 8
1971	Apr 18	Dinghy, saved dinghy and 2
		Inshore Rescue Boat, of Llandudno, gave help
	27	Yacht Club rescue boat, escorted boat
	June 6	Yacht *Idler*, gave help and landed 1
	20	Cutter *Sea Foam*, saved cutter and 2
1973	Aug 3	Yacht *Spindrift*, saved yacht and 2
	6	Dinghy, with outboard motor, saved dinghy
	Nov 17	Fishing boat *Girl Betty*, saved boat and 2
	Dec 12	Speedboat, saved boat and 2
1974	Feb 13	Fishing boat *Selontieum*, gave help
	May 26	Landed an injured cliff climber

Vincent Nesfield Relief Lifeboat

	June 26	Cabin cruiser *Tel Jay*, landed 2
	Sep 20	Speedboat, escorted boat
	Nov 6	Fishing boat *Untouchable*, gave help

Lilly Wainwright Lifeboat

1975	Aug 10	Fishing boat, gave help
	16	Yacht *Tessa*, saved yacht and 2
	24	Pleasure boat, landed 1

Dec 12   Dinghy, landed a body

1977   Apr 12   Power boat, saved boat and 1

June 10   Motor cruiser, landed 3

July 23   Yacht *Rossekop*, gave help

Aug 4   Yacht *Dyllys*, saved yacht and 2

Sep 28   Yacht, saved yacht

Vincent Nesfield Relief Lifeboat

1978   July 8   Boy stranded on cliff, gave help

Lilly Wainwright Lifeboat

1979   July 8   Yacht *Bowie*, gave help

1980   July 20   Yacht, saved yacht and 2

Sep 21   Yacht *Stoux*, saved yacht and 2

1981   Aug 30   Yacht *Falcon*, gave help

Nov 29   Motor cruiser, gave help

Dec 30   Llandudno ILB on service to cabin cruiser *Surf Power*, stood by boats

1982   Aug 29   Yacht *Honey Dew*, gave help

Sep 27   Fishing boats, escorted boats

1983   Oct 24   Motor boat, saved boat and 2

1984   Apr 26   Yacht *Wychcraft*, gave help

Vincent Nesfield Relief Lifeboat

1985   Apr 21   Yacht *Juno*, gave help

May 24   Speedboat, saved boat and 1

Lilly Wainwright Lifeboat

1986   Aug 14   Sailing dinghy, saved boat

1987   June 4   Fishing boat, gave help

Aug 20   Yacht *Iolanthe*, escorted yacht

Calouste Gulbenkian Relief Lifeboat

1988   May 27   Person stranded on cliff, gave help

July 1   Fishing vessel *Sarah Jane*, gave help

24   Yachts *Spindrift* and *Zazoom*, escorted

Aug 12   Dinghy, saved boat and 2

1989   June 21   Yacht *Tranquility*, saved boat and 1

Nov 5   Dinghy, gave help

Lilly Wainwright Lifeboat

1990   June 19   Yacht, gave help

24   Catamaran, gave help

July 1   Colwyn Bay Sailing Club rescue boat, saved boat

Andy Pearce Lifeboat

1991   Apr 16   Motor boat *Dizzy Lizzy*, saved 5

June 2   Motor boat *Julia Ann*, gave help

14   Man fallen from pier, gave help

July 8   Rowing boat *Piper 3*, saved boat and 2

27   Cabin cruiser *Mary Four*, gave help

Aug 21   Motor boat *Sally*, escorted

26   Motor boat, saved boat and 4

Sep 29   Cargo vessel *Marga*, stood by vessel

1992   Jan 5   Motor boat, saved boat

May 14   Speedboat *Whoosh*, gave help

23   Yacht *Starrynight*, gave help

June 18   Cargo vessel *Residu*, stood by

July 12   Yacht *Tarantelle*, gave help

Aug 22   Yacht *Crimson Rambler*, gave help

25   Man overboard from speedboat, gave help

Oct 3   Sailboard, escorted board

1993   Mar 12   Trawler *Solitaire*, with mine in net, took off crew and gave help

13   Assisted RN Bomb disposal team with detonation of mine

June 15   Small power boat, landed 4

Fisherman's Friend Relief Lifeboat

Aug 4   Motor Boat *Moody Blue*, gave help

Andy Pearce Lifeboat

Nov 4   Motor boat, gave help

1994   Feb 12   Fishing vessel *Ellen M*, two persons and craft brought in

Apr 16   Motor cruiser *Quest*, two persons and craft brought in

June 18   Cabin cruiser *My Only Vice*, saved boat and 2

Yacht *Lady Amron*, saved boat and 2

26   Fishing boat *Rosie and Jim*, three persons and craft brought in

July 31   Man in sea, took out police officers

Aug 6   Yacht *Ellen Kelly*, one person and craft brought in

26   Motor boat *Golden Kestrel*, four persons and craft brought in

Sep 25   Speedboat in tow of Llandudno ILB D-432, escorted boats

Nov 12   Fishing vessel *Iona*, saved vessel and 4

1995   Feb 11   Yacht *Blaze*, landed 3 and craft brought in

July 1   Sick man onboard yacht *Frenchleave*, saved boat and 2

Yacht *Denise,* saved boat and 2

8   Motor cruiser *Sea Quest*, landed 2 and craft brought in

30   Speedboat, three persons and craft brought in

Aug 6   Diver support craft, five persons and craft brought in

Oct 30   Motor boat, stood by boat

1996   Apr 26   Cabin cruiser *Kumfi Two*, three persons and craft brought in

May 2   Man stranded on Llandudno pier, stood by

June 25   Yacht *Cela Viendra*, two persons and craft brought in

Aug 29   Cabin cruiser *Almodes*, two persons and craft brought in

Nov 15   Cabin cruiser *Horizon*, saved life-raft and 2

1998   May 23   Cabin cruiser *Day Dreamer*, three people and craft brought in

June 6   Yacht *Elber Lady,* one person and craft brought in

7   Motor boat *Sea Fury*, ten people and craft brought in

July 6   Sailing dinghy, gave help

Aug 9   Diver support craft *C. Diver*, six people and craft brought in

Dec 6   Unknown vessel, recovered wreckage

14   Yacht *Shim Shall*, landed 3 and craft brought in

Peggy and Alex Caird Relief Lifeboat

1999   Apr 16   Cabin cruiser *Odyssey*, escorted craft

Andy Pearce Lifeboat

July 4   Yacht *Enchante*, Four people and craft brought in

17   Yacht *Baremka*, Five people and craft brought in

Aug 21   Cabin cruiser *Alexandra*, saved 1

Nov 14   Speedboat *Sea Ray*, Four people and craft brought in

Dec 13   Yacht *Emma Louise*, Four people and craft brought in

2000   Apr 16   Speedboat, landed 5 and craft brought in

Nov 24   Workboat *Sea Witch*, two people and craft brought in

Dec 31   Angling boat *Huntress 2*, gave help

2001   Feb 4   Fishing vessel *Osprey*, four people and craft brought in

26   Fishing vessel *Mercury*, two people and craft brought in

June 30   Yacht *Fantasia II*, stood by

Oct 13   Yacht *Carpe Diem*, 2 people and craft brought in

27   Yacht *Ellidi*, one person and craft brought in

Dec 14   Sick crewman on drilling vessel, landed 1

2002   Jan 27   Injured crew member aboard yacht *Victoria Conway*, escorted craft

Feb 25   Motor boat *Silent Water*, escorted craft

Sep 10   Sail Yacht *Sea Spray*, landed 1 and craft brought in

Dec 14   Angling boat *Silent Waters*, nine people and craft brought in

2003   Mar 29   Motor boat, landed 2 and craft brought in

May 11   Pleasure fishing vessel *Northern Rover*, saved craft

18   Yacht *Thrilla*, gave help, initiated tow to Beaumaris ILB

June 21   Motor boat, five people and craft brought in

July 17   Yacht, two people and craft brought in

19   Yacht *Blue Osprey*, two people and craft brought in

Aug 8   Powerboat, gave help

2004   Mar 16   Fishing vessel *Patricia D*, escorted craft

Apr 17   Yacht *Cilla*, three people and craft brought in

May 4   Yacht *Shakara*, saved craft and 3

July 22   Yacht *Wychwood*, Escorted craft

24   Catamaran *Esmerelda*, landed 2 and saved craft

Aug 12   Yacht *Tara*, Three people and craft brought in

Oct 16   Yacht *Mjolner*, saved craft and 2

Dec 16   Coaster *Arklow Freedom*, gave help – stood by then escorted vessel

2005   Mar 26   Powered boat *Emotion*, two people and craft brought in

Lifetime Care Relief Lifeboat

July 10   Fishing vessel *Merry Fisher*, three people and craft brought in

17   Yacht *Pisces*, two people and craft brought in

Andy Pearce Lifeboat

Sep 5   Powered boat, five people and craft brought in

Nov 14   Powered boat *Wasp*, two people and craft brought in

2006   Mar 18   Yacht *Manana*, landed 4 and craft brought in

Apr 8   Yacht *Daydream*, three people and craft brought in

14   Yacht *Dulcinea*, five people and craft brought in

June 10   Diver support craft *North Wales Divers*, five people and craft brought in

17   Yacht *Dawn Trader* two people and craft brought in

Nov 8   Fishing vessel *Oysker* escorted a vessel

2007   May 4   Passenger vessel *Princess Christine*, gave help and escorted craft

24   Angling vessel *Celtic Fisher*, 9 people and craft brought in

June 23   Powered boat, escorted craft

Powered boat, landed 2

Sailing dinghy escorted craft

Yacht *Tonga 2*, escorted craft

July 9   Yacht *Sea Griffin*, gave help - freed anchor

Yacht *Sweet Jane*, stood by

28   Yacht *Glogg*, one person and craft brought in

Aug 5   Yacht *Aquila*, landed 3 and craft brought in

11   Yacht *Mahita,* two people and craft brought in

11   Yacht *Pride of Marvic*, two people and craft brought in

2008   May 24   Yacht *Four Bells*, landed 2 and craft brought in

July 10   Yacht *Therapy*, landed 3 and craft brought in

25   Yacht *Silver Marine*, two people and craft brought in

Aug 2   Yacht *Firebrand*, two people and craft brought in

25   Yacht *Elinora*, three people and craft brought in

26   Yacht *Odyssey*, saved craft and 2

Sep 7 Sail training vessel *Greater Manchester Challenge*, 17 people and craft brought in

9 Yacht *Sea Time*, two people and craft brought in

20 Powered boat *India Jay*, three people and craft brought in

28 Powered boat *Bull Beggar*, three people and craft brought in

30 Yacht *Predator*, two people and craft brought in

2009 Apr 4 Powered boat, one person and craft brought in

June 13 Yacht *Wasp*, three people and craft brought in

July 13 Powered boat, two people and craft brought in

24 Yacht *Laura*, two people and craft brought in

2010 May 2 Jet ski, landed 1

Jet ski, craft brought in

July 3 Yacht *Grace*, two people and craft brought in

17 Yacht *Comrades*, one person and craft brought in

Oct 9 Yacht, four people and craft brought in

Fisherman's Friend Relief Lifeboat

2011 Feb 16 Yacht *Proteus*, four people and craft brought in

Apr 8 Powered boat *Elise*, five people and craft brought in

Andy Pearce Lifeboat

June 4 Yacht *Swiss Made*, one person and craft brought in

June 26 Inflatable dinghy, landed 2 and craft brought in

Aug 14 Kayaks, landed 2 and craft brought in

Sep 24 Yacht *Athena*, four people and craft brought in

2012 Apr 3 Cargo vessel *Carrier*, lifeboat unable to give assistance

May 17 Work vessel *Tuskar*, rendered assistance and four people assisted

July 15 Yacht *Larkin*, rendered assistance and four people assisted

Aug 22 Yacht *Yo-Yo*, rendered assistance

Work vessel, rendered assistance

2013 Apr 18 Yacht *Helgi 2*, rendered assistance and five people assisted

Mary Margaret Relief Lifeboat

2014 May 4 Powered boat, rendered assistance

Andy Pearce Lifeboat

June 1 Powered boat, rendered assistance and three people assisted

Aug 13 Yacht *Larrikin*, rendered assistance and rescued 5

Oct 24 Powered boat, rendered assistance

2015 Apr 12 Yacht, rendered assistance saved 2

19 Yacht, rendered assistance and rescued 5

May 27 Yacht, rendered assistance

July 12 Fishing vessel, rendered assistance

2016 Feb 29 Fishing vessel *Lady Gwen*, rendered assistance and 1 person rescued

Apr 27 Windfarm vessel *Tenacity*, rendered assistance and saved 9

May 14 Power boat, rendered assistance and rescued 2

25 Yacht, rendered assistance and saved 2

June 3 Powerboat *Angel of Beaumaris*, rendered assistance and 2 people assisted

5 Yacht, gave help and 3 people rescued

July 1 Yacht *Bluewater Fox*, rendered assistance and 3 people assisted

25 Yacht, gave help and 2 people rescued

Sep 30 Yacht *Shadowfax*, rendered assistance

Oct 3 Fishing vessel, rendered assistance

2017 Jan 20 Yacht *Joie de Vivre*, rendered assistance and rescued 1

June 20 Yacht, rendered assistance and rescued 2

July 18 Yacht *Sandpiper of Sleat*, rendered assistance and assisted 9

Aug 17 Yacht *Esprit*, gave help and rescued 1

William F. Yates Lifeboat

Aug 23 Speedboat, rendered assistance and rescued 3 [LB training out of Poole]

Motor sailer, rendered assistance and assisted 2 [LB training out of Poole]

Sep 23 Motor yacht, gave help [LB on passage]

Nov 9 Fishing vessel *Proper Job*, rendered assistance and rescued 1

Dec 4 Windfarm support vessel *Kitty Petra*, rendered assistance

2018 May 27 Person cut off by tide, rendered assistance

June 30 Yacht *Footsie*, gave help and saved 4

July 21 Fishing vessel *Nicola Faith*, gave help and saved 1

27 Yacht *Last Tango*, rendered assistance and rescued 2

Aug 6 Capsized kayaker, rendered assistance and landed 1

Sep 30 Yacht *Greengoose*, stood by

Oct 1 Fishing vessel, rendered assistance

10 Fishing vessel *Nichola Faith*, rendered assistance

30 Fishing vessel, rendered assistance

2019 Feb 21 Yacht, rendered assistance and rescued 2

24 Yacht *Trappasser*, rendered assistance

Mar 17 Kayaks in difficulty, saved 2

F • Personnel summary

Honorary Secretaries*

John Williams	1861-1876
George J. Felton	1876-1890
Rev John Raymond	1890-1922
J.J. Marks**	1922-1939
J. Roberts**	1922-1933
J.E. Hallmark	1939-1948
Thomas Taylor	1948-1978
Lt Cmdr Edward (Ted) Yates	1978-1994
Lt Cmdr John McDonald	1994-2000
Brian Fisher	2000-2003
Captain Marcus Elliott	2003-

* Lifeboat Operations Manager from 2002
** Joint appointment until 1933

Coxswains

Hugh Jones	1861-1876
Richard Jones	1876-1890
John Hughes	1890-1904
Edward Griffith	1905-1917
John Owen	1918-1930
Robert (Robin) Williams	1930-1940
Trevor Davies	1940-1953
Edward (Ned) Lloyd Jones	1953-1960
Gordon Bellamy	1961-1970
Meurig Davies MBE	1971-1994
Ian (Dan) Jones MBE	1994-2009
Robin Holden	2009-2011
Graham Heritage	2011-

Mechanics

James Jones	1933-1944
Caradoc (Crad) Harris	1944-1970
Robert (Bob) Jones	1970-1982
Adrian Dunkley	1982-1987
Lionel Collis	1987-1999
Leslie (Les) Jones	1999-

Second Coxswains

Richard Jones	1861-1876
Edward Jones	1876-1887
Richard Thomas	1888-1890
Thomas Parry	1890-1893
John Williams	1893-1904
John Owen	1905-1917
John Jones	1918-1923
Robert (Robin) Williams	1923-1930
Trevor Davies	1930-1940
Edward Goodey Jones	1940-1944*
[No Second Coxswain	1944-1947]
Edward (Ned) Lloyd Jones	1947-1953
Samuel Lloyd Jones	1953-1960
Gordon Bellamy	1960-1960
Ernest Lloyd Jones	1961-1964
Meurig Davies	1965-1971
Christmas (Chris) Jones	1971-1981
Anthony (Tony) Frost	1981-1988
Lt Cmdr John McDonald	1989-1989
Ian (Dan) Jones	1989-1994
Robin Holden	1994-2009
Graham Heritage	2009-2011
Dave Davis, Tim James and Danny Jones**	2011-2015
Robin Holden**	2011-2014
Timothy (Tim) James	2015-

* with breaks for war service
** joint Assistant Coxswains

The passage crew who brought the 13m Shannon William F. Yates to Llandudno were, left to right, Luke Heritage, Tim James (Second Coxswain), Graham Heritage (Coxswain), Les Jones (Mechanic) and Mike Jones. (Nicholas Leach)

G • Coxswains

1861-1876 • Huw Jones

1876-1890 • Richard Jones

1890-1904 • John Hughes

1905-1917 • Edward Griffiths

1918-1930 • John Owen

1930-1940 • Robert (Robin) Williams

1940-1953 • Trevor Davies

1953-1960 • Edward (Ned) Lloyd Jones

1961-1970 • Gordon Bellamy

1971-1994 • Meurig Davies MBE

1994-2009 • Ian (Dan) Jones MBE

2009-2011 • Robin Holden

2011 • Graham Heritage

H • Mechanics

1933-1944 • James Jones

1944-1970 • Caradoc Harris

1970-1982 • Robert (Bob) Jones

1982-1987 • Adrian Dunkley

1987-1999 • Lionel Collis

1999 • Leslie (Les) Jones

PAGE 192 • Llandudno lifeboat crew on 23 September 2017: seated, left to right, Dr J.J. Green (Chairman and Lifeboat Medical Advisor), Ralph Hughes (tractor driver), Robin Holden (Lifeboat Training Coordinator), Dan Jones (Head Launcher), Tim James (Second Coxswain), Graham Heritage (Coxswain), Les Jones (Mechanic), Myfanwy Jones (Lifeboat Visits Officer), Mike Knowles, Paul Moreton and Alun Pari Huws (Deputy Launching Authorities); standing, left to right, Aled Williams, Simon Hajahmed, Phill Howell, Dave Jones, Les Howell, Barney Baker, Bert Williams, Robbie Shields, Dave Davis, Nigel Forrest, Luke Heritage, Keith Charlton, Mike Jones, Steve Howard, Danny James, Dave Roberts, Sue Davies and Kelsey Byrne. Not pictured are Marcus Elliott (LOM), Andy Jones, Adam Finch-Saunders, John Roberts, Ian Appleton, Vinny Hill and Chris Martin.

J • Ladies Guild

A Ladies Committee was first formed at Llandudno in 1895 by Lady Mostyn for street collections and flag days, and between 1914 and 1919 almost £2,000 was raised, an impressive sum, particularly as it was during the Great War.

The Guild in its current form came into being in 1922 under the Chairmanship of Mrs Marks, with Mrs Raymond as Secretary. Mrs Raymond had been recently widowed following the death of her husband, who was Honorary Secretary from 1890 until his death in 1922. During Mrs Raymond's tenure, until her death in 1931, over £5,000 was raised.

Several of the Guild's prominent members and officers were wives of Branch officers or committee members although, interestingly, in 1922, both Mrs Raymond and Mrs Marks, wife of the Rev Marks, who was also Honorary Secretary, were invited to join the Branch committee. Successive Lady Mostyns have been presidents of the Ladies' Guild.

The three main roles in the Guild were Chairman, Secretary and Treasurer, but there were other roles. Many office holders were in post for years and several were recipients of RNLI honours, including one life governorship. Mrs D.J. Wilkes, Secretary

of the Guild for many years, was awarded a Gold Badge in 1947 and made an RNLI Honorary Life Governor in 1964. Mrs Joan Gibson joined in 1933 and served until her death in 1993. Mrs Edith Bellamy, now well in her 90s, completed fifty years of service in 2015 and remained a volunteer.

In 1994 the Guild had a particularly good year, raising £22,000 in the year, helped by running a small kiosk on the pier. Until 2011, during Lyn Brown's tenure as secretary and Sue Eite's tenure as Treasurer, activities were concentrated on the promenade, where Andy Pearce was on display on most Sundays during the summer months. In 2011, following problems with the caravan on the promenade from which souvenirs were sold, the RNLI decided to open a shop in Lloyd Street (below), which became one of the RNLI's busiest.

While some individual Guild members have been named, there are many others who have contributed. The work of the Ladies Guild and its principal officers has been a valuable and integral part of the station's operation. In January 2018 the Guild was wound up and a new Supporter's Group started under the leadership of Sue Perkins.